Infantry Colonel

INFANTRY COLONEL

Brigadier George Taylor
CBE, DSO & Bar, KHS

Published in 1990 by
The Self Publishing Association Ltd
Lloyds Bank Chambers,
Upton-upon-Severn, Worcs.
A MEMBER OF

in conjunction with
Brigadier George Taylor
22 Deans Court,
Milford-on-Sea, S'hampton.

British Library Cataloguing Publication Data
Taylor, George
Infantry Colonel
1. World War 2. Military operations by allied forces 2. Korean War. Army operations by Great Britain. Army
I. Title
940.54

ISBN 1 85421 085 8

Produced and Designed by The Self Publishing Association Ltd
Printed and Bound in Great Britain by Billing & Sons Ltd, Worcester

Contents

Dedicated to the Infantry Soldiers of the British Commonwealth and of the United States of America

Acknowledgements

My thanks must go to John Elliot for editing my manuscript, which was written by me in Germany, at the end of World War II, whilst events were fresh in my memory. He was able to polish sentences and make a number of alterations and additions for which I am extremely grateful.

History of The 43rd Wessex Division by H. Essame.

Story of Seventh Battalion, The Somerset Light Infantry by J.L.J. Merdith.

FOREWORD

There have been many books about military operations written by generals and other senior commanders who have had the responsibility for strategic planning and for the movement of large armies operating on a broad scale.

But there have been fewer books by officers in command of, and in close personal touch night and day with, infantry soldiers in the front line . . . officers who have been at the 'sharp end' of the battle, having to make rapid decisions and issue clear orders whilst in direct contact with the enemy.

Few, if any, Battalion Commanders acquired more experience or had a finer record than George Taylor in the campaign in NW Europe during World War 2, in which he brilliantly and bravely led the 5th Battalion The Duke of Cornwall's Light Infantry in a number of decisive battles in Normandy, Holland and Germany.

As Intelligence Officer of the Battalion I was perhaps in as good a position as any to witness not only his great courage and inspiring leadership, but also the care with which we reconnoitred and planned every attack or defensive engagement, in order to minimise casualties.

Though he himself was a highly trained professional soldier, he recognised the potential worth of the volunteers and conscripts who formed the majority of the Battalion and he succeeded in turning them into a formidable fighting unit.

Despite the strain and stress of enemy shelling and the inevitable casualties, morale under George Taylor remained high, for his personal courage and genuine concern for all those under his command inspired in all ranks a deep loyalty and affection for their Commanding Officer.

Methods of training and military tactics may have changed during the last 50 years as new weapons have been invented, but the qualities that characterize a good leader have probably remained constant.

I am very pleased that this gallant soldier has decided to write his memoirs, for they will surely reveal some of the secrets of his brilliance and deserved success as an Infantry Colonel.

Sir David Willcocks CBE, MC, MA, DMus, DLitt
(formerly Intelligence Officer, 5th Bn. DCLI)

PREFACE

The sight of my father, handsome, tall, dark figure in the green of the 8th Irish (The King's Regiment) probably determined me to be a soldier. I was only four years old, and he was battalion commander of the 8th Territorial unit and senior partner in a prosperous wood-turning mill.

The Taylors were the owners of a coal mine near Wigan. It is said they were noted for their good relations with the miners and not averse from meeting them man to man at sport and over a pint. The Taylor's in the 18th Century bought Standish Hall in Lancashire. Miles Standish, who had lived there, was the only soldier on the Mayflower on its epic journey to America.

Like many Lancashire people, we were Catholics who had determinedly held on to the old faith of England during the time of Elizabeth I.

My father, Thomas Taylor, died after an operation at the early age of 42, leaving my mother, Florence, a widow at 35 and six boys to bring up. Her outstanding characteristics were her kindness and steadiness.

My boyhood was a happy one in those days before the First World War at Blundellsands, on the Lancashire coast, some 10 miles north of Liverpool. Never more so than our yearly visit to Trefrew, in North Wales, where we had a summer holiday cottage.

Hostilities with the local village lads started in the first week of the holidays and the young Taylor boys took on considerable odds . . . the battles raging all summer, with suitable armistices for time off for such less exciting events as family picnics, country walks and rides in pony and trap.

Our engagements were fought out mainly in the mountains – our weapons of bows and cloth headed arrows, sticks and clods of earth against the more hazardous, at times armoury of stones and sometimes air guns of the Welsh opposition. From these rough encounters I was to grasp an almost instinctive knowledge of military tactics.

After attending St Francis Xavier's, a day school in

Liverpool run by the Jesuit Fathers, the time came for me to follow my elder brothers to boarding school at St Cuthbert's College, Ushaw, Durham, the excellent Northern school where boys of all classes were trained for the priesthood, although my brothers and I belonged to the limited category of non-clerical students. Ushaw, established during the Napoleonic period, had a great tradition and great moral standards. One of the things I learned there was not to think about one's fellows so much against a background of class, but more on their intrinsic worth as human beings. This was due to the fact that the pupils came not only from some of the oldest Catholic families in the land and very solid middle class homes, but also from more humble backgrounds, many of them from Durham miners' cottages.

Although Ushaw did not play rugby, the game had become my first love, I had picked up the game mainly by playing in the public school matches organised by the Waterloo club during the Christmas holidays. I was very fast for my size; I could do the 100 yards in 10.1 secs, and soon worked my way into the Waterloo first XV and then into the Lancashire team as a wing forward.

Waterloo at the time had a crop of Internationals: H.G. Periton, who captained England, Roy Foulds, Stan Wallens, the two Meikle brothers, and Scotland's S.B. McQueen and J.P. McArthur. Waterloo has what is probably the unique record of supplying at least one international to the England XV every year between 1924 and 1958.

Although spending a few early years in the cotton trade on the Cotton Exchange, which had begun its decline after the General Strike of 1926, I had not forgotten my ambition to be a soldier. I joined the Cheshire Yeomanry and shortly after was commissioned into the 7th Bn, The King's Regiment, a TA unit, later to distinguish itself as the 40th Royal Tank Regiment with the New Zealand Division and 9th Australian Division in the desert in 1942. Sir Geoffrey Beazley, the CO, sensibly recruited most of the officers from the Waterloo Rugby Club. I thoroughly enjoyed my service as a Territorial, and eventually decided to try for a regular commission. I often wonder how I got through my examination at Sandhurst. My guardian angel must have played a very full part.

Besides some haphazard reading, my main preparation was a six week course with a crammer, a Mr Redway, in London. It is no doubt due to his efforts that I passed the exam.

I was gazetted to the West Yorkshire Regiment and joined them in Northern Ireland in February, 1929. Early on, I had several clashes with my company commander. He was a veteran of the Great War who had obviously fought with great gallantry and endurance, winning the DCM and MM. The first of these differences was about minor tactics, whether or not you led with your light machine gun sections or your rifle sections when advancing in fog.

It was foolhardy of me to take on this experienced veteran and the result was inevitable. He reported me to the CO, Lieut Col Boyle, saying that my standard of training was poor. It was decided that I should do an extra months field training with another company.

This nearly resulted in me getting a rugby international cap. I was already fit, but a further month of long marches and movement across country and on the long slopes of the beautiful mountains of Mourne, often carrying a heavy Lewis gun to give the gunner a rest, tuned me to a peak of supreme fitness.

At the time, Lancashire had reached the final of the County Championships. We met Middlesex at Twickenham, and a hard game ended in a draw. I was at the top of my form in this match. So there was a replay. Middlesex were then a star-studded side, with players from all the countries of the United Kingdom and some from the Dominions. Lancashire were beaten in a very fast game. Middlesex were captained by W.W. Wakefield.

I had no recollection of most of the second half, because when a scrum was 10 yards from our line, Powell, the powerful Welsh scrum half, broke through, due to an error on my part. In despair, I threw myself backwards and brought him down a yard from the line, but I suffered bad concussion. I was delighted to hear a week later that I had been picked to play for the Barbarians on their Easter tour of Wales.

The Baa-Baas that year included the great Scottish Oxford three-quarter line G.P.S. MacPherson, W.M. Simmers, and E.C. Taylor: half-backs J.C. Powell and Herbert Waddell, later to command the only flame-throwing tank unit in the Second Army in Normandy, and forwards who included the great J.M. Bannerman, H.S. MacIntosh, my two friends the Ludlows, and J. Farrell, a most amusing Irishman.

The match against Swansea brought home to me how physically hard the Welsh forwards were, men from the mines and steel mills. Tackling them was like crashing into concrete. I must have played well, because MacPherson said to me after the match, "Shame on you, George, if you don't get an England cap next season." Alas, it was not to be. Despite the efforts of the Army Rugby Union, headed by Major General Basil Hill, to keep me at home for a couple of years at the Regimental depot, orders came through from the War Office that Second Lieut G. Taylor was to proceed with his unit to the West Indies.

As it was, only half the battalion went to Jamaica; I and the remainder embarked on HMT *Naivsha* for Bermuda, where we were to spend two delightful years of activities consisting more of the ceremonial, sporting and social activities than of active training for war.

One night, after a good dinner, I met Kipling and had a most delightful talk with him about soldiers and soldiering, about which he had written so much.

Life in Bermuda was much too social for us young officers; dances under a tropical night sky in the roof gardens of the palatial hotels; drinks at the yacht club; invitations to receptions on board visiting British luxury liners and American yachts.

There was, fortunately, a facility which prevented me from embarking on too great a slide into the gay and carefree life: a small but splendidly stocked garrison military library. There I spent a considerable time reading works on military history. I became a great admirer of the writings of Colonel Henderson and studied his "Stonewall Jackson" with great interest. Henderson had, in fact, written this military classic when he had been in Bermuda some 30 years before, spending his leaves researching in the United States, going over the ground of those epic and terrible battles of the Civil War.

In the late twenties, a spate of war histories, autobiographies, and biographies had been published: Churchill's *World Crisis*, the official histories of France and Flanders, the Gallipoli and Mesopotamia campaigns, Wavell's Palestine campaign, Dennis Reitze's *Commando*, the writings of Fuller, and last, but not least, the works of Liddell Hart. All had a powerful effect on me. The Australian *Official History of the War* gave me a feeling of great admiration for the fighting qualities of the men from the Antipoder. Little did I realise then that 21 years later I was to have the privilege of commanding Australians and New Zealanders in battle. They lived up to my high opinion of them as soldiers.

The great majority of my brother officers had little interest in war. To the young, it was something remote that would not happen in their time, though they would not be averse to taking part in a small "North-west Frontier" type of battle.

Senior regimental officers, who, judging from their decorations must have been gallant men of action, would hardly mention the last war and the campaigns in which they had taken part. Thus, we younger men had only an inkling of the true atmosphere of war, with its resistant medium to human will be design, where the simple becomes extremely difficult; because fear, doubt and fatigue stalk the field, one is racing to do something against time, often dependent upon the help of others. In addition, accident or the friction of human personality can quickly throw the whole design out of gear.

Later, I was to coin a phrase which perhaps expresses the heart of the matter: "In war, if a thing can go wrong, it certainly will. It's better if it comes under the heading 'Murphy's Law'."

The attitude of most of our seniors was probably a defensive mechanism of the mind: "A great war will never happen again in our time; therefore, let's forget the grim, bloody business." Undoubtedly, they, like most people, had been affected unconsciously in their minds by peace propaganda and the general feeling of pacifism in Britain. If Hitler had been able to wait another 10 years there might not have been much resistance.

A fresh wind had started to blow, at least in the West Yorkshires. Lieut Col Harold Franklyn was appointed to command the first Battalion. A tall, slim figure with a scholarly stoop, he was without a doubt one of the top three or four battalion commanders of the early thirties. His clear-minded enthusiasm for soldiering was obvious, and like a lot of great men he was easy to talk to.

By now, we were beginning to look forward to a change of scenery: Ismailia, the Canal Zone. And life there was vastly different from the paradise isle where we had wiled away the last two years. In Egypt, the British Army of that period was at its best. Morale was high and training, in many ways, was as realistic as limited means would allow. Fierce but friendly competition existed between all units both in work and play. The GOC, General Sir Jock Burnett Stuart, was an outstanding general.

Franklyn, our new colonel, knew his job well and in a short time the battalion had a reputation second to none in the Egyptian Command, which included two Guards battalions. The secret of his success was that he took all ranks into his confidence, talking to the whole battalion from time to time. Thus, he was able to kindle a great spirit of enthusiasm.

The British Army has always been heavily officered, which has often meant that the ability of the warrant officers and senior NCOs was not fully used. They therefore tended to become somewhat wooden in their attitude, concentrating their efforts on weapon training and the minutiae of drill. Franklyn changed all that and many of them became real leaders of men and excellent minor tacticians. The proof of his success was to show years later in the fighting qualities exhibited by the West Yorkshires in the desert and in the jungle against the Germans, Italians and Japanese.

Training in Egypt was thorough and rigourous, testing fit men to the limit of their physical endurance. The techniques of the long night approach march across the desert and night or dawn attacks were constantly practised; we became masters of night movement and felt practically naked if asked to move across the desert in daylight.

Handicapped though we were by a general lack of equipment and training funds, the colonel nevertheless, by a judicious mixture of imagination and the practical, produced training schemes of interest and realism; the use of Army lorries as assault craft; the desert representing the sea and a line of steep hills the hostile coast; the armour, I remember the tanks once attacking a position under cover of a dust storm, shades of the battle of Gazala (Desert War) when Rommel attacked in a desert storm. The use of transport aircraft in an infantry assault role, also an exercise in which the planes came down on the flat desert just outside enemy machine-gun range; the infantry quickly disembarked and then moved in to attack. Similar to the German use of transport aircraft in the coming battle of Crete. And now today we are moving rapidly into a time when the helicopter will be an essential part or even dominate the battlefield.

The desert was used to test our initiative and foresight. Platoons and sections, under their young commanders, made forced marches across the Sinai Desert, having first to plan the march and make all the administrative arrangements.

It was Colonel Franklyn who was to pioneer the character-building "Outward Bound" system, which tests small groups of boys and young men against the forces of nature, rugged country or the sea.

The brigade was commanded by Brigadier Tim Pile, later to become commander of Britain's anti-aircraft defences during the Battle of Britain and for the rest of the war. His chief staff officer was Sandy Galloway, who was to rise to Lieutenant General and under whom I was to have the privilege of serving after the war.

The redoubtable Lieut Col Bernard Law Montgomery was commander of one of the three battalions in the brigade 1st

Battalion, The Warwickshire Regt. He had a high reputation for his military knowledge. His expression: "Damn it, it's in the book . . . I wrote it" referring to the Manual of Infantry Training, was typical of his professional knowledge and character. We did not think he was such a good battalion commander as Harold Franklyn.

To join this galaxy of talent in the brigade, on one hot summer afternoon came Freddy de Guingand, one of the greatest staff officers, the British Army has ever produced. I was detailed to meet him at Ismailia Station. A medium sized figure with a pale face and a warm smile greeted me from the carriage window. He became Franklyn's adjutant, and a high powered combination they were. Freddy had spent most of his soldiering in Central Africa. He had tremendous confidence in himself, and was gifted enough in speech to put over his progressive ideas in a masterly way. The Brigadier called him, "my little Napoleon".

During the winter, Freddy worked to pass the Staff College entrance examination. It was both his first and final effort to surmount this stiff hurdle, because of the age limit of 33. He was also sorely tempted by the offer of command of a battalion of the King's African Rifles.

He made the right decision. He took the examination and passed by a few marks. But he was to pass out top of the Staff College and go on to fame and glory.

Later, as Montgomery's Chief of Staff, he was the perfect foil for the great commander of the Eighth Army. I believe it was the experience of commanding a battalion in Egypt that made the future field marshal concentrate his sharp intellect on his own failure to achieve outstanding high morale in his unit.

CHAPTER ONE

The Panzers from Russia

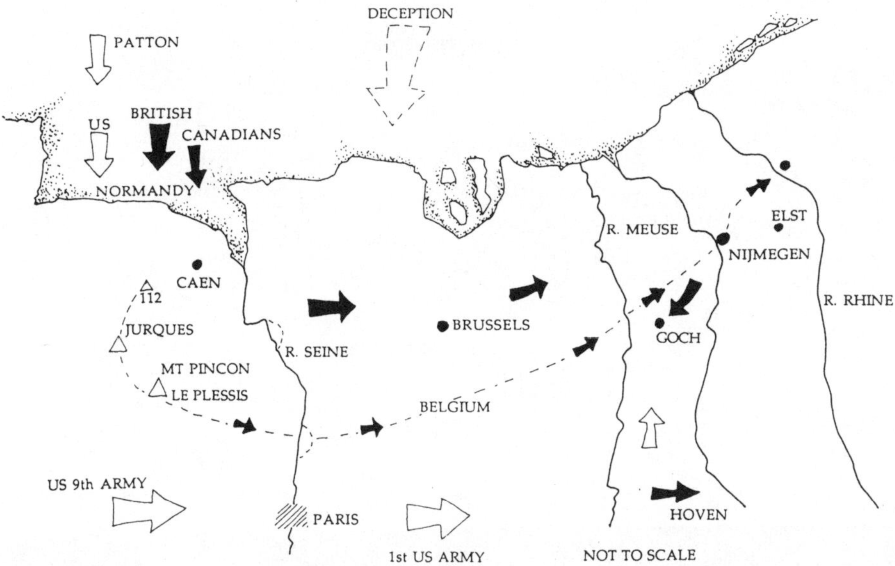

The 5th Battalion in the UK just before 'D' Day

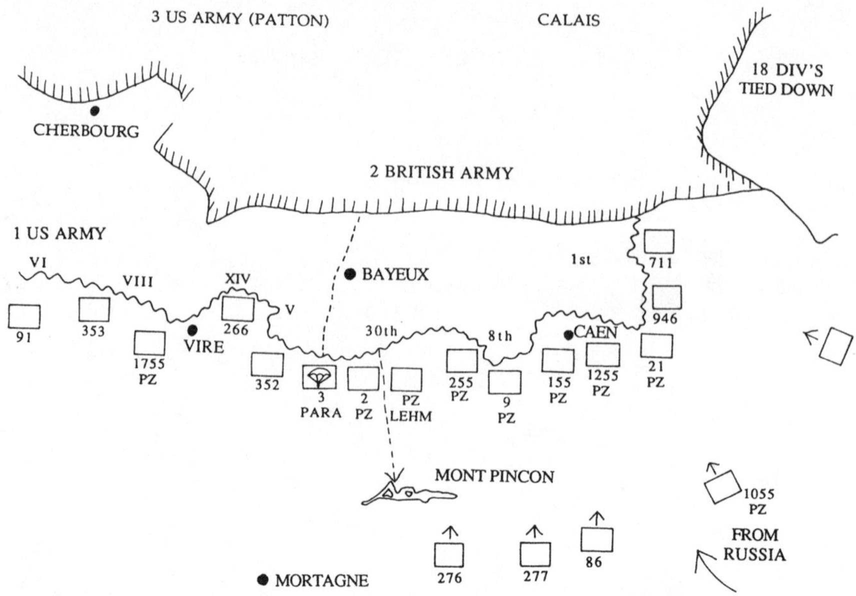

A Patrol in typical Normandy BOCAGE

Now the long sojourn in Kent was over. For four long years the cold inhospitable beaches of Lydd and the tangled woods and contoured hills swept in winter by the Siberian winds from the east had been the training ground for the men of Cornwall, Somerset, Wiltshire, Dorset and more recently the men from the heart of England, the Worcestershire's, whilst in the earlier period dog fights in the air had raged overhead.

We did not realise how the terrain around our main training area Stone Street closely resembled the fields of Normandy, where we were to engage the enemy in many crucial battles.

In that exhilarating early summer of 1944, 43rd Wessex Division was at last on its way. From the ports of Newhaven, Southampton, and London we had swept on to the Normandy beaches already in Allied hands, in spite of the great storm which had blown forebodingly between June 19 and 22.

Under Brigadier Peter Essame MC and veteran of World War I, consisted of the 1st Worcestershire, 7th Somerset Light Infantry, and the 5th Duke of Cornwall's Light Infantry, with its supporting Arms of 179 Field Regiment Royal Artillery and sub Units of Anti tank Guns RA Machine Gunners and 8th Middlesex Regiment, Royal Engineers, REME detachments and Field Ambulances RAMC.

All through the long day of June 26, the brigade had waited tensely but patiently, in its assembly area of Ruqueville. There had been a momentary stir of excitement when reconnaissance parties were called forward to meet the Brigade commander in the vicinity of Cheux, a village eight miles to the west of Caen.

There the 15th Scottish Division, flanked on the right by the 49th Division, with the 43rd Division providing the dual role of covering from the left and filling in from behind, was steadily with great courage boring its way forward. But the opposition had been tough and casualties heavy. The Scots were up against élite troops the Wafen SS young volunteers officered by war experienced leaders. They were disposed in depth in the thick hedged Bocage country and lurking behind them having arrived from the Russian Front was II SS Panzer Corps consisting of the 9th and 10th Panzer Divisions.

After seeing his fierce but disjointed counter-attacks fail after the Allies' D Day offensive on June 6, Rommel had changed his tactics and committed his armoured reserves in a determined attempt to cordon off the bridgehead.

Our time had come. The Wessex men were to provide the much needed reinforcements to relieve the Scots. Now we were to find out the true value of those long, hard years of training in the Weald. I was at that time 2nd in command of the 1st Bn Worcestershire Regiment in the brigade.

At midnight, 5DCLI were ordered to take over the 9th Cameronians, who were located immediately south west of Cheux, and the Somerset's were to move up on the left. We Worcestershire's were to stay back in reserve.

I watched the DCLI move off, led by their commanding officer, Lieut Col J.W. Atherton. His civilian role as a lawyer belied the skill as a military tactician of this tall, lean man. For a time he had commanded the Divisional Battle School that had been established in 1942 on the golf course at Sandwich and through which had passed all the platoon, company and section commanders who would lead the division in battle.

As he went by, I wished him luck. He replied sombrely: "I'll need it, George."

Little did I know then, that in less than two short weeks, I would have his job, with Atherton and his successor dead.

With some men on foot and others mounted on gun carriers, anti-tank guns, and jeeps, the DCLI led the brigade off into the dark night. The roads were covered in mud from the recent downpours, and the march was a nightmare.

For the first time, the men were experiencing their first whiff of battle. The night reverberated and flashed to the continual firing of guns; and in the half-light of dawn, they were greeted by the sight and smell of dead cattle, with their bloated bodies and woodenly stiff, legs, and burnt out tanks, both British and German. All of which, with the roughly hewn crosses by the wayside marking the graves of the fallen, reminded everyone that this was no "exercise in Kent", though the lovely hills and quaint villages were strongly similar.

Though long, sweeping fields of grain clothed the bottom of the verdant valleys, with their orchards, but mostly thick hedges, ditches and tall trees, small fields, made up the true Normandy bocage.

The roads running into the ancient sturdy stone villages were steeply banked, and the rich earth was drained by a myriad of sparkling streams. Fine defensive country for the infantryman with his easily concealed mortars and machine guns but restrictive and difficult for tanks and attacking infantry.

It was daylight by the time the battalion arrived on the reverse slope of the hill that dominates Cheux from the north. An extraordinary panorama of modern warfare was spread out below them; on the left was a mass of tanks of a British Armoured brigade; intermingled with them bustled the infantry men, moving about, digging in; gun-pits were being excavated for the 25-pounders, and already some of the artillery were moving in.

To the right, flame throwing tanks, supported by small groups of infantry were flushing a thickly hedged area for snipers, small parties of sturdy but pale faced prisoners, were being brought in.

Along the muddy track, a constant stream of vehicles was moved in the opposite direction to the toiling infantry; ambulance cars driven with an air of urgency; Jeeps fussing about carrying officers of all arms, cheerful or tense according to temperament; 15 cwt trucks lumbering through on miscellaneous missions of supply.

Artillery shells from friendly guns passed overhead, whispering their message of death; hostile mortar bombs burst in ugly black splodges on the distant crest, sometimes dropping among the tanks and the sleepy-eyed but apprehensive, infantry with a horrible crushing sound. And all the time could be heard the distant crackle of small fire arms.

The Scots had driven the enemy back several thousand

yards in a series of vicious engagements. But now they were exhausted and depleted in numbers. The takeover by the DCLI had to be completed in daylight.

The battle hardened. Jocks enjoyed their moment as they were relieved by the new campaigners; their quips and cynical remarks as they passed the incoming men were not of the type that inspired confidence . . . "Taking over the line" was an experience new to the men who had spent most of the war in the fields of Kent, but in the days ahead it was to become a familiar operation, and one to be practised in training. I was worried when I heard that it was to be a daylight 'take over'. Safer to do it at night.

Cheaux was to teach them an early lesson in the procedure. A misunderstanding resulted in 9 Cameronians, who had captured part of the village at great cost the previous day, withdrawing their 17 pounder RA anti-tank guns, without realising that those of 5DCLI were still stuck somewhere in a mighty traffic jam.

The situation was confusing, the Cornishmen began to dig themselves in. Major AFC Kitchen, commanding C Coy decided to make a reconnaissance of the area allotted to him – an orchard on the right flank – and, to his horror, found it full of Germans!

B Coy, meanwhile, were making themselves at home in an orchard of the high banks of a sunken road. They were heartened by the rumble of tanks approaching along the road at 9 am.

Six monsters appeared and turned into the orchard "Nice to have armour in support" someone said. "Pretty decent guns on them. Funny camouflaging though. MY GOD, they're German!"

The stark, black crossed on the turrets of the Panther tanks were all too evident, the first action of the war for 5DCLI and for 43 Division was about to begin. The leading tank turned the corner and ran head on into the unsuspecting troop of Royal Artillery 17 pounders, on their way to relieve the non existent 6 pounder troop who had been reported to be further up the road. With a few shots it knocked all four guns out.

The other five tanks wheeled into the orchard that served as the headquarters for D Coy, commanded by Major John Fry, and halted literally on top of the slit trenches in which the men lay. A frightening first taste of battle, but men of Cornwall rose to the occasion magnificently. Fry rallied his company and the stalking of the Panzers began.

The two battalion 6 pounder anti tank guns had been taken out, so Captain H. Jobson, D Coy 21/c, brought in his piat teams. As the tanks edged forward towards Battalion HQ, Cpl Ronan and Sgt Hicks opened up on them from behind. Trucks and carriers of the soft vehicle column burst into flame as the tanks picked them off at 50 yards range, like a Sunday morning duck shoot.

Col Atherton, alerted by the din, arrived from the village. Seeing one of the gun crews knocked out, he stepped in as loader to keep the gun firing. A burst from on the Panthers 88s killed him and the rest of the crew instantly.

But the tanks had run themselves into difficulty. The rear end assault by the hand held Piat bazookas was having devastating effect; one Panther turned tail and fled, hit three times by the Piat of Lieut Prowse, of 17 Platoon; it got away, badly damaged and with the crew obviously shaken up.

Sgt Hicks knocked out another from close range; two turned a corner to be confronted by Pete Blackwell, of C Coy and his Piat party, one was destroyed and the other turned over in its desperate effort to escape, like a cornered beast. The fifth tank fell victim to a 6 pounder; much to the surprise of the gun crew, it brewed up at 100 yards range.

In their first action the DCLI had accounted for five tanks and their battle hardened SS crews in less than half an hour, in an action fought at speed and with great ferocity. But the stark reality of war had been brought home to them, they had lost 20 men killed and wounded and their CO among the dead.

Two factors won the day for the battalion: one was the great leadership and personal example set by Major Fry. He had suffered the humiliation of being chased round the orchard by one of the Panthers, leaping in and out of the slit trenches, in the terrifying cat and mouse game. But all the while he continued to shout encouragement and instructions to his men. The other was the horrifying action by one of the tank crews. They had opened fire on two stretcher bearers carrying a wounded man to company HQ, then, callously, they had driven over the soldier on the stretcher . . . It had served as a great stimulant to the man's comrades. So, the DCLI were in the war at last, and they had set a high standard in the Division to live up to in the next 11 months.

With gallant Atherton gone his number two, Major Dick Janes, a young Territorial officer took over. The battalion, though undoubtedly surprised by the first shock of war partly due to the confused daylight take over, had stood firm and had fought hard. The men's confidence in themselves and their weapons particularly the short range but lethal Piat grew stronger.

The PIAT hand anti tank weapon which the battalion used with success

Reports of the action spread like wildfire through the Division, and morale was enhanced. The battalion remained in the Cheux area for three days enduring heavy mortaring and shelling. In addition the Germans new terror weapon the Nebelwerfer a multi-barrelled mortar was constantly active, but after a little experience one found that it's terrifying bark was worse than it's bite.

It was during this period, that for the first time, we began to realise how important to us hearing was in the body's mechanism of defence. Like the line sweats of the 1st World War, the man with sensitive ears could pick up out the mortar bomb or shell from which to take cover from those he could afford to ignore. Some never managed to acquire the art and would duck or dodge unnecessarily.

Fighting continued around the Brigade in earnest. I was kept back from the Worcester's first action, as they took the village of Mouen in a workman like attack under the CO Roy Harrison, instead of being tempted to use a covered approach, attacked across a corn field behind a barrage using a lot of smoke . . . thus surprising the enemy. I came forward to congratulate him, whilst they were consolidating.

Armoured Carriers of the Batallion moving towards the Front

On June 29, a fierce armoured encounter took place on the Brigades right watched in a battle of Waterloo manner by large number of top brass gathered on the high ground north of Cheux. The tide of battle was flowing gradually, but inevitably, towards Hill 112, a ridge dominating the valley of the River Odon and Caen, towards the north east, it was said that whoever held the Hill 112 held Normandy.

On the night of June 29, 5DCLI were relieved by a battalion of Dorset's from 130 brigade, and next morning advanced 2,000 yards to the hamlet of Coleville, which they were to hold as a firm base or pivet for armoured operations by our tanks.

Coleville overlooked a prominent crossroads which was used by many units for bringing up supplies, ammunition and reinforcements. Consequently it attracted a great deal of hostile mortar and shell fire, zeroed in on the hung dust cloud which constantly shrouded the spot.

Losses within the battalion were reduced by strict discipline of movement and by the building of protective covering over the slit trenches.

In the late stages of the divisions' training in England, the use of houses for defensive purpose was frowned upon. So during those early days in France, command posts were usually set up in a trench, which proved to be unsuitable because of cramped conditions and the difficulties of communication under fire. Though there was some bombed out buildings that could be used to practise street fighting in.

We were quickly to learn that the best company or battalion command post was a good strong building with cellar, care being taken not to occupy the isolated house which tended to draw the fierce fury of the enemy's fire.

Here, in the battalion command post (advanced battalion HQ), the CO would dictate the course of the battle, surrounded by his entourage of intelligence officer, signals officer, pioneer officer, scout platoon officer and support commander, with their respective detachments. When there were no convenient buildings, advanced battalion HQ would operate from a newly dug foxhole on a ditch running alongside the road! We devised a relief system that after a successful attack and once we had consolidated, my Second in Command Major Andy Martin would come forward to take over from me – so that I could get a short sleep. Without this system I doubt whether I would have lasted the campaign.

The Normandy weather of those late June days was hot, and the sickening stench of dead cattle pervaded the air. A minor plague health worry for the medical authorities. At the same time, we began to get a number of medical cases officially termed "battle exhaustion". Some of these were undoubtedly men whose minds had been disturbed by intensive shell fire. But others were the weaken brethren who lacked the necessary strength of will to keep going when exhausted by lack of sleep and tested by shelling and mortaring and all the other unpleasantries of war.

Later I made it a rule that exhaustion cases were only to be evacuated to B Echelon (transport lines) where our good Doctor Dickie Williams, treated then with sleeping pills and in a few days they were back with their Companies.

I emphasised the value of sleep before battle and we developed a drill to ensure this (battles are often fought by tired men). The worst cases were men who seemed to care only for the safety of their own skins, and who became cunning in their methods of avoiding dangerous duties, but there were very few in the DCLI or Worcestershire's.

All ranks soon became adept at recognising the genuine cases, from the malingerers, and reacted in a very healthy manner against this small minority of stand-backs. "Battle Exhaustion" cases became rare. The brigade carried out active training and patrolling by night; much information to feed our gunners was gleaned from this and from the stream of French refugees passing through out lines.

It was near Carpiquet that we witnessed for the first time bomber command operating in close support of the Army. The blasting of the enemy to the north of Caen by hundreds of Lancasters and Stirlings was a sight never to be forgotten, and the effect on our men's morale was most heartening. Patrols discovered that the enemy had evacuated the village of Fontaine Etuopefour, south of the Odon. But the Germans still held Hill 112 in strength with an outpost on the forward slope.

On the morning of July 3, orders came the 5DCLI were to occupy Fontaine, which, after the Canadians had taken Carpiquet, would provide a firm divisional base for the attack on the Hill.

After experiencing the discomforts of Colleville for four days, news of the move came as a relief to the battalion. With the Canadians poised for their attack on Carpiquet, it was a vital that any advance be concealed from the enemy as much as possible.

It was decided to move forward under cover of darkness, to be fully dug-in and consolidated by dawn. The troops, therefore, were to move along the line of the railway to Verson, and the transport was to follow by road once the village had been occupied.

The Brigade ordered the Cornwall's to take via Verson, Fontaine Etuopefour which had been retaken by the enemy from another battalion. Bill Gorman vividly describes this advance to this strongly built stone village which clustered round it's church and Chateau.

> "The battalion left Colleville at midnight: there was no moon and it was very dark. At first, the advance went easily, with men moving in single file over the open heath and at a steady pace. All was quiet, except for the shells from both sides that swished overhead through the still July night. Occasionally, a salvo would fall unpleasantly close, and those nearest ducked involuntarily as the deadly splinters whined menacingly into the distance. But what had started off as a pleasant night time stroll deteriorated into a nightmare as the Cornish men reached the railway track. On places, the rails had been torn up and jagged fingers of twisted steel bit into unweary ankles; shell holes pitted the track, and bodies littering the banks looked like a grotesque, lurking enemy.
> Broken telegraph poles had fallen across the rails. But worst of all was the wire. It was everywhere – telegraph wire, railway wire, signal cable, all tossed up on the track like tangled knitting wool. And in the darkness men stumbled, sweated, tripped, and cursed there way forward, now more concern with

the obstacles in their path than with the sudden flash and burst of falling mortar bombs or the tracer flying in thin pencil lines above.

Near Verson, the ordeal ended, and the battalion paused for a while to reorganise. They began the decent into Fontaine Etoupeher. Entrance into the village was an eerie experience. By now, there was a pallied moon, and in the dim grey light the place looked like a ghost town.

The relics of battle were there a derelict tank, with one track spread out behind it like a giant entrail: broken ammunition boxes, a twisted gun, shattered houses, and shell splattered walls. The men moved in cautiously, but no one, friend or foe, was there to greet them. By dawn they were dug in and concealed."

Surprised prisoners brought in next day confessed that patrols had visited the village twice in the night and were completely unaware that, under cover of darkness, a whole battalion had taken up residence there.

The Canadians, however, were finding things more difficult. Their first attack on Carpiquet, supported by a terrific barrage, had failed, mainly because of deeply dug-in and well concealed Tiger Tanks. Although the observation posts pinpointed them accurately enough for the British and Canadian gunners, the 25 pounder shells made little impact on the stubborn foe.

The enemy's skilful defensive use of his thick skinned Tigers combined with skilfully concealed mortars and machine guns was something of a tactical surprise and was causing the Allies endless difficulties and were beginning to decimate the carefully trained infantry of the rifle companies on whom the bloody burden chiefly fell. The German defensive system was some 5 to 10 miles in depth based on their experiences of the battle of Passchendaele depth and the counter attack being the essence.

One of the Brigades more precarious pastimes during this

period was the nightly mortar run, which entailed 18 carriers thundering down the road in darkness towards Verson to put down harassing fire on the Germans.

Shoots were initiated by the brigadier, who held a conference each morning to outline "target for tonight": in attendance would be all battalion mortar officers and the Lieut-Colonel Harrison, CO of 1 Worcester's, commanded the shoot on the second night. On the previous missions, 18 mortars had fired 1,800 bombs in 10 minutes from a little orchard just south of Verson, a precarious position affording little or no cover.

"But such was the nature of the ground that nothing better could be found. The suspected target was 1,500 yards away, and with 1,800 flashes in 10 minutes emanating from an area 200 yards square, it was amazing that we got away before retaliation started.

"I have never seen 18 carriers move so fast as the three mortar platoons returning that night to Colleville".[1]

The next afternoon, the recce party spent two hours looking for an alternative position, but the orchard was the only piece of sunken ground in the area.

It had suffered the full fury of the enemy's vengeance. Bomb craters were everywhere, giving it the appearance of a lunar landscape. Of the numerous empty bomb cases let by the battalion mortar men in the previous night's escapade, not one remained intact.

Stokoe the support Coy Commander said: "I think Col Harrison and Jock Bannister shared the feelings with mortar officers that the nights shoot should be called off. This however was far from being the brigadiers opinion he at this time was very keen on the use of mortars as a battery and ordered us to proceed at 0200 hours and repeat the dose of the previous night.

I remember Captain Bannister, mortar officer of the Worcester's pointing out to the brigadier that our mortar position was straddled with craters and must be well known to the Boche."

---

[1] To quote Jock Bannister.

The brigadier replied cuttingly: "We are not afraid of craters Bannister."

The mortars were in position again by 1 am, and a feeling of foreboding hung heavy in the air. "I cannot remember an hour going so slowly as that to H-hour, at 0200 hours," said Stokoe. "You could have heard a pin drop".

The night was ripped asunder and turned to day by the continuous flashes as another 1,800 "eggs" were delivered to the enemy in 10 more mad minutes. "I remember the barrel of our gun glowing like a cigarette end from over heating, added Captain Stokoe. "Just as we got our last mortar out and on to the carrier, we heard the familiar sound of a Nebelwerfer opening up. We did not wait to see where the bombs landed."

The battle zone, however, was not without its compensations. We were in the centre of rich farming land, and to supplement the inevitable compo rations were poultry, eggs, butter and vegetables in abundance. The men also made their acquaintance with the rough cider of the country and the fiery calvados, or apply jack a spirit made from apples.

A draft of 60 men, including several Canadian officers, arrived to bring 5DCLI back to strength, and on July 8 news came that the battalion was to re-occupy Fontaine Etoupefour. The Canadians had taken Carpiquet and had now turned their attention on its airfield.

CHAPTER TWO

The Crown of Thorns

The stage was now set for the whole division to swing into action. The fighting of the next few days was to reach a standard of sustained ferocity equalled only, perhaps, by the Reichswald and Siegfried campaigns months later. With the 4th and 5th Wiltshire battalions advancing on their flanks, 4 Somerset's, supported by Churchill tanks and heavy artillery, were instructed to storm and capture Hill 112 on July 10.

The battle for Hill 112 going on in the distance

While 129 Bde were thus engaged, 130 Bde 7 Royal Hampshire's, 4 and 5 Dorset's, plus 7 Somerset's would take Eterville and Malto and push towards the River Orne.

The hill dominates the two valleys of the Orne and Odon. The approach to its summit from the north is a gentle incline over 1,500 yards of open country. At the top was a field of corn and a small orchard, surmounted by a tree-lined hedge; in the course of the coming holocaust, this orchard was to become known to us as "Calvary Wood". To the

Germans, the shall shattered, splintered trees after the battle were to represent another Easter analogy, the "Crown of Thorns".

On the steeper reverse slope were two moderately sized fields, and running up from Esquay, to the south west, was a curiously shaped re-entrant, as though someone had spooned away a portion of the hill. After several days of overcast, the morning of July 10 dawned bright and clear. A good omen for the attack, we hoped.

The Somersets' plan seemed a sensible one: the two leading companies each with a troop of tanks, were given the limited objective of dealing with the enemy outpost positions on the forward slope; the two reserve companies also with tanks, would leap-frog through to capture the small diamond shaped wood.

They attacked with great courage, but the carnage was fearful. Bursting shells and mortar fire decimated their ranks, but they hit back with every weapon available to them: Brens, Stens, rifles, grenades and tank fire.

The enemy outpost position was captured. The two anti-tank guns and their crews were wiped out, and many Germans lay dead in their slit trenches.

But the Somersets' casualties were so heavy that the plan to capture the orchard with the reserve companies was abandoned. The problem was that for a short time too many men had been exposed under tremendous artillery and mortar fire. No doubt the plan had been based on World War I trench tactics, whereby the first wave would capture a line of trenches and shelter in them while the second wave would leap-frog through to occupy the next line.

In this case, however, there were only a few scattered slit trenches available for shelter, thus casualties of high proportions were inflicted on the Somerset's; 12 officers and 400 men. Surely, the long 1,500 yard approach called for a night attack, but the decision against it might have been influenced by the great success of the Worcester's daylight attack on Mouen.

There had been an astonishing argument over an open wireless line between General Thomas, who wanted the attack at night, and Brigadier Essame, who advocated a day assault.

The General, threatened to remove the brigadier; fortunately, Lieut Col Roy Harrison, CO of 1 Worcester's, saved an embarrassing situation by attacking in daylight through a cornfield, under cover of a smoke-screen, catching the enemy completely unawares.

In Mouen following the failure of the Somersets' attack, the situation in front was critical, in the face of the enemy counter-attacks to the west. Although the German outposts had been destroyed, their main defences were cleverly sited on the reverse slopes of the hill and in the village of Maltot.

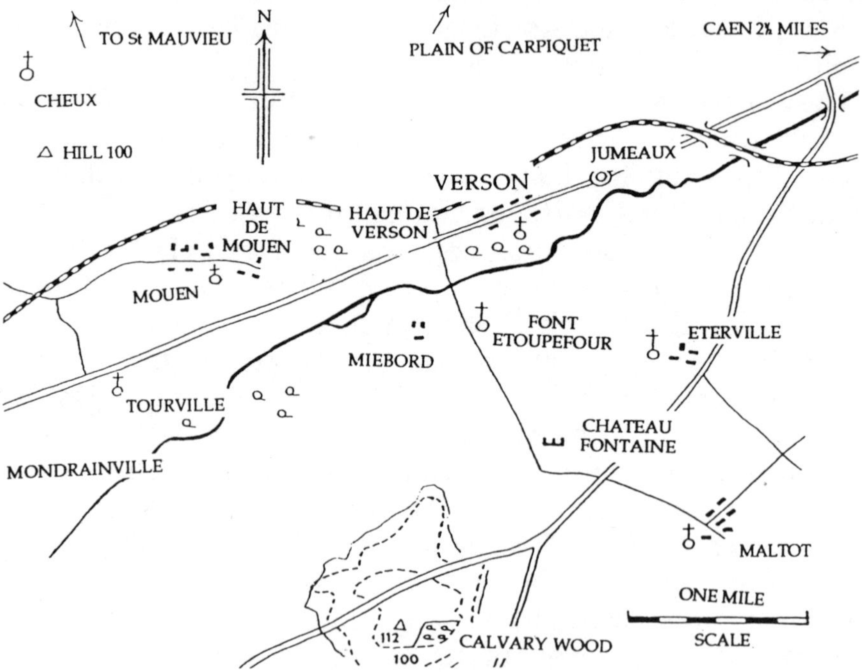

LEGEND 1. *The valley of the ODON is steep and wooded.*
2. *The high ground at Carpiquet, Jumeaux, Eterville, Hill 112 and Haut de Mouen overlooks the saddle formed along the road from Haut de Verson to Verson*

The general called a meeting of his brigadiers in the Chateau Fontaine. It was vital to him that Hill 112 was captured, and he now had only one battalion in reserve, 5th Duke of

Cornwall's, who were located near Fontaine Etoupehour.

HILL 112

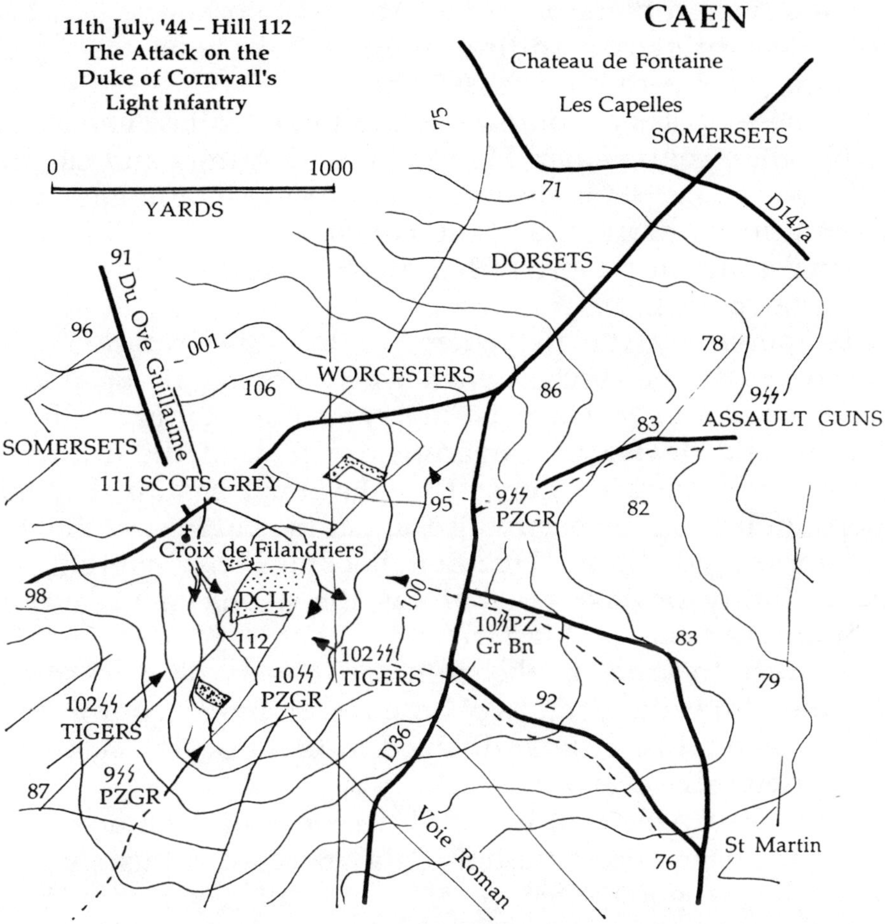

CORNERSTONE OF THE
NORMANDY CAMPAIGN

In the late afternoon, it was decided to put 5DCLI under the command of 129 Brigade to help secure the top of the hill, Brigadier Essame told Dick James of this decision, in the big house near the church at Fontaine Etoupefour. I attended this conference. Time was of the essence, as the attack was to be pushed home as the light faded, supported by tanks. Essame asked James how much he required to work out details.

Slightly flushed of face, the CO calmly worked out the time factor on a piece of paper. At least two hours, was his reply. The brigadier adding another half hour for good measure, fixed zero hour at 20.30 hour.

On these occasions, time is always the relentless enemy of the battalion commander. He has to think calmly and clearly of the essentials, while dealing with outside interference and interruptions, draw the right conclusions from his own reconnaissance and those of his subordinates, and take stock of all viewpoints.

Hampered by the vagueness of local information, his decision has to be reached often when moving at speed in a carrier or scout car. He must marry in the armour with the infantry and devise the covering fire plan of the artillery, mortars and machine guns. Then he must ensure that his troops undaunted by enemy fire, are at the battle start line by the appointed hour. Heavier becomes the weight of responsibility on his shoulders as the hands of his watch seem to turn faster and faster.

We were to learn, in the grim and bloody days to come, that the time allowed, two hours and practised for this process, should be at least doubled in times of war against a strong defensive position.

James, like Atherton, his predecessor, had been a lawyer before the war and, although only 26 he used his shrewd legal mind to good effect in planning military tactics. Like Atherton, too, he had served a term commanding the divisional battle school during training in Kent.

Now, after a final recce of the daunting task awaiting 5DCLI his order of battle was drawn up: two assault companies, C Coy right, B Coy to the left, would provide the initial thrust, with A and D in close support.

An extensive fire plan was laid on to soften up the defences and the tanks would deploy in the rear of the two assault companies. Things went well on the right when the operation started at 20.30 hours, (it was still daylight) with C and D Coys making ground quickly along the right. But B Coy, on the other flank, were caught in the open by heavy machine gun fire and suffered appalling casualties.

Their CO, Major Gerald Vawdrey, was killed trying to keep the attack going. A Coy managed to work round on the left, and Lieut Doug Ritchie, with 9 Platoon, cleared the machine guns, killing most of the crews taking the rest prisoner. Of Major Vawdrey's company, only 40 men survived.

The enemy had beat a hasty retreat from the small orchard on the flank, one platoon of D Coy, caught up in the excitement of battle, followed their commander, Lieut Carmelli, beyond their objective and down into the valley in hot pursuit of the Germans.

Carmolli, a Canadian serving with the British army under the Canloan scheme, was killed, along with most of his men. Perhaps a foolish action, but Major Bob Roberts, A Coy commander, was to write later: 'No one who saw it will ever forget their courage and determination.'

Roberts and Major Fry, of D Coy, decided to hold the line of the hedge, running roughly halfway through the wood, and bring in the shattered remnants of B Coy. With the light now fading and the Germans retaliating with shell and mortar fire, the position had become precarious. Dick James arrived to assess the situation and ordered the Carrier Platoon to come up immediately to strengthen the position in the orchard.

The companies had not much chance to dig in, and accurate artillery and mortar fire were taking a heavy toll. The Anti-Tank Platoon lost a complete crew and one 17 pounder gun was put out of action. Under this fire, the enemy had launched a counter-attack. But, said Major Roberts, "We had no difficulty in repulsing the infantry, the fire discipline being first class and both companies giving

Boche absolute hell. It was grand to hear the section commanders shouting out their orders 'Hold your fire, chaps, until you can see the b . . . . . . s eyes!' It did fearful execution."

After repulsing this rabbit-punch attack, the Cornwall's dug in furiously among the roots of the fruit trees. About midnight, the Germans came again, with armour and infantry. The tanks approached the edge of the wood, raking it with machine gun fire from east to west, while their rifle men tried to infiltrate round the right flank.

The Cornishmen crouched low in their slit trenches, but as soon as the tanks withdrew they were up and at them with Bren and Rifle fire. The German Infantry were quickly despatched by D and C Companies. The performance was repeated throughout the night as the Germans sought desperately to retake the Hill. James showed just why he had been given such great responsibility at so young an age.

Said Roberts: "The CO was magnificent. He set an outstanding example to everyone by his personal courage, endurance and irrepressible spirit. The position we were in would have taxed the most seasoned of troops, and we were still rather green, but for him, I don't know what might have happened."

Just before dawn, came word that a squadron of Scots Greys were being sent into relieve the pressure, with a company of the 1 Worcester's. The tank arrived just before first light, cheering the beleaguered men immensely. We the Worcester's were positioned just to the left of the DCLI and I strongly advocated that we help with a company.

James asked the Squadron Commander if he would push through and clear the enemy from the rear end of the wood and also deal with a machine gun that was worrying D Coy. This they did in style, but at enormous cost. It seemed that every 88 and mortar that the Germans had opened up on them. The Greys lost five Shermans in 10 minutes.

Although the tanks were drawing the fire away from the DCLI, the increasing casualties were making it apparent that unless the Worcester arrived soon, the Cornwall's would be over run by sheer weight of numbers, if the Germans chose to put in another attack. I being second in command of the

Worcester's had suggested that we reinforce with a Rifle Company.

The field gunners were lending magnificent support in breaking up the enemy bid to form up down the hill and on the other side of the wood. George King, commanding 7 platoon, acted as OP, with Dick James correcting the fire of the gunners. It needed a cool head, for with the Germans only 150 yards away, an error on his part would bring a salvo down about their ears.

Just such a tragedy happened, when one fell short of 7 platoon, killing King and Sgt Hill. It was after Colonel James had ordered Major Roberts back to arrange evacuation of the wounded and to see about getting the company of Worcester's that the news began to infiltrate round the battle-weary men: "The CO's had it!"

He had climbed a tree to direct the artillery fire when a burst of machine gun fire had hit him in the neck. The young lawyer who had been such an inspiration to all was dead. When the first burst of tracer had just missed him his body guard shouted "come down sir . . ." James replied "I am coming," but it was too late.

Now with the Colonel dead the splendid fighting spirit that had sustained the battalion through many hours of grim and deadly struggle began to wane.

Someone shouted: "Retreat! Retreat!" Who it was will ever remain a mystery. One theory is that it was a German. Men began to drift to the rear and the contagion spread and considerable number reached the position held by the 4th Somerset's, where the latter's Colonel C.G. Lipscomb, with the help of Gorman, Willcocks and Roberts rallied them and led by Roberts and Fry got the remnants back to their original positions on the top of Hill 112, which says a lot for their brave powers of recovery.

For a time there was a lull in the bombardment, but at about 3 pm the Germans put a smoke-screen down the right. The four tanks appeared on the left and began firing into the trees. With little head cover, the casualties again began to mount rapidly among the men of the DCLI. The anti-tank gunners were unable to depress their guns sufficiently for an effective reply, but Lieut Bellamy managed to move one of his 17 pounders out into the open to have a crack at the tanks.

They were barely able to get off one round before a tank shell put paid to most of the crew. Recalled Major Roberts "To give some idea of how depleted the battalion had become, just before I was wounded I made a tour of the companies and the effective strength was 126, although many wounded were still lying where they had fallen or been hit in their slit trenches: some were still firing, though very weak for loss of blood and fatigue".

Brigade headquarters came on the air midway through the afternoon and asked for an officer to go back to Brigadier Essame to give an exact account of the situation.

The adjutant, Captain Gorman, took advantage of another lull in the fighting to carry out the order. He told the brigadier that the position held by the battalion was unsound and further delay in withdrawing the survivors would lead to the final destruction of 5DCLI.

Meanwhile, the short respite for the tired, dazed and greatly depleted garrison had ended. The wood was now being swept by an intense storm of mortar bombs and shells. It was the most clearly defined target for all the hostile weapons that could be brought to bear on it from east, south and west.

Enemy tanks with self-propelled guns in close support now appeared on the scene, raking the area with machine gun fire and solid shot. Their onslaught brought no reply: the battalions anti-tank guns were now silent, as most of the crews were among the casualties; there were few undamaged Piats and little ammunition to go with them; most of the officers and the NCOs had been killed or wounded, and of the three companies only about 60 men were left unscathed.

The fighting 5th had been in action for 14 consecutive days and for the last 21 hours had been grimly battling in this inferno on top of the hill. From the moment it had bravely taken the position, the battalion had been constantly counter-attacked with tanks and infantry of the elite 10th SS Panzer Div.

It was difficult to estimate when one counter-attack finished and another started, but is thought there were a least 10; all but the last were driven off at heavy cost to the Germans.

There was nothing more the Cornwall's could do. Flesh, blood and nerves have their breaking point, and that had nearly been reached. Major Fry realised the survivors were on the point of being overwhelmed and sent a message asking for permission to withdraw.

Back came the reply: he should return to explain the situation. As the only senior officer remaining. Fry felt he could not possibly leave the men in their dilemma, so he made up his mind to save what he could of the remnants of the battalion in the death trap of Calvary Wood.

The plan was shouted to each company: "We will clear out of this when the smoke comes down. Each man for himself. Keep well separated." Shrouded by the smoke, they fell back to the road, some 100 riflemen, many of them wounded, and what was left of the gun crews, and carriers. The officers of Battalion HQ Bill Gorman, David Willcocks, Max Stock, Lieut Birchenall and Captain Stokoe, the Mortar Platoon Commander rallied the dazed and depressed survivors and a defensive locality was formed near the headquarters.

Gorman and Lieut Willcocks, later Sir David Willcocks, Director of the Royal School of Music, were later to receive the MC for their cool headedness and gallantry in this battle.

* * *

I have often wondered what my tactics would have been had I been in command during the battle of Hill 112. The battalion's objective, the little orchard spanned an area of just 300 sq. yards, of which 5DCLI held one half. At one time, there were over 350 Cornwall's in this small space; surely it would have been better to have tried to hold it with just one rifle company and anti tank guns, backed up with tanks positioned on the northern slope.

Then, as casualties mounted, reserve platoons could have been fed in during lulls. We now know that the Panzer grenadiers suffered very heavy casualties and if the above method had been used we could have perhaps won this battle of attrition, but this is hindsight.

The capture of Hill 112, with its excellent observation advantages, could have forced the Germans to retreat from Caen. As it was, the attempt to hold the narrow salient on the top of the hill had failed and the battalion had suffered a disaster in the heavy casualty figures, 16 officers and 320 other ranks, the death of its gallant CO, and the savage blow to its morale in being forced to withdraw.

But like a phoenix from the ashes, there were to rise from the survivors stout hearted officers, NCOs and men who were to form the basis of a most formidable fighting machine that was often to be in the spearhead of the Allied thrust in carrying the war from Normandy into the heart of Germany.

Ironically, what is perhaps the biggest tribute to the fighting qualities of the Cornishmen who resisted so gallantly and died in Calvary Wood is contained in the official account of the German division involved in the action on Hill 112: "In the forefront of the battle, in the area of Evrecy-Baron, Avenay-Veux, Hill 112, SW of Caen, will always be associated with the name of the division. For there, the division fought greatly superior numbers, and always elite troops on what was to become known as "Cornwall Hill".

After the war we found out that the Panzer Grenadiers Infantry at the end of the battle were on average down to some 20 men per company.

CHAPTER THREE

The New Command

I was summoned by the brigadier, and walked down the road, shell fire had splattered it with leaves and branches from the tall trees. I felt as if I was dreaming it seemed so unreal. Essame was obviously a worried man. "Go George and take them over and kick them up the backside!" This was out of character as Peter Essame was a man of generous spirit.

I had no intention of doing this as I knew what a gallant fight they had put up. I found the officers and men who had survived one of the most terrible battles of the war shocked but unbroken in spirit.

Some 300 reinforcements arrived from many regiments, including 50 from 4th Bn DCLI. They were tired, dusty and hungry, and the first thing we did was to give them a good meal. I shook hands with each one and said a few words of welcome. Everything depended on the quality of these men an they were not to disappoint us in the traumatic times to come.

I wrote a special Order of the Day: "On taking command of this fine battalion, I would like all ranks to know how honoured I feel. Our immediate task is to reorganise, absorb our new comrades, and then go forward and finally destroy the enemies of our country and of all decent men."

One of the great difficulties that has to be faced after taking heavy casualties is that of selecting suitable private soldiers for promotion to NCOs. A small reserve of trained potential material was gone, and few non-coms had come forward with the newcomers. I instituted a system of short courses in the hope of bringing men up to the required standard, and much later in October the divisional battle school from our training days in Kent was reconstituted. But in each case, neither the time allotted not the numbers trained could meet the demand fully. The German system of NCO courses lasted six months and were very thorough and they were taught to think at two levels higher than their rank.

I had two main intentions in rebuilding the battalion into a crack fighting unit: one was to establish an elite company that I could use as a spearhead, or reserve, the other was to have a scout platoon for reconnaissance. The man I chose to lead this group of shock troops, to become A Coy, was a former Army bugle boy named Harry Parker of the Oxford and Bucks LI.

Harry, medium built with blue eyes, was one of those natural warriors that Britain seems to create. Still in his twenties, he had risen to the rank of major after being commissioned on the field at Dunkirk, having won the Military Medal. An outstanding tactician, he was to fulfil the role in every way.

Two officers and 20 NCOs and men from the 4th Bn volunteered to be our scouts and the platoon was to prove its worth in seeking vital information. It was also to cut down our officer casualties, as NCOs, down to lance corporal, were to carry out dangerous scouting missions with courage and efficiency. Nowadays, every battalion has its reconnaissance platoon. It is of specially great importance because of the wide dispersion in fighting formations.

I spoke to all officers and stressed that in any attack they must learn how to position themselves. They were to move in the centre of the danger area, and not in front of it, a remark attributed to a general in the American Civil War. This was to apply particularly to platoon commanders, especially at the start of an attack until the moment came when they must lead their men in the final charge.

I told them that we would attack in greater depth than was customary in most battalions, and that *unless* we had time to locate the enemy with a good degree of accuracy, we would attack with only one company, backed by the maximum firepower.It was realised that unless one had been in close contact with the enemy for several days we would know very little about his dispositions and that we would have to fight to make him show his hand.

If this method failed, then the enemy would probably

have disclosed his hand anyway and a fresh plan could be instituted for the strong reserve.

After some of my battle experience lectures to Army Units in the late eighties a number of Officers mentioned that on 'Exercises' they are told too much about the enemy dispositions.

It could be said that we were to attack on too narrow a front, but in battle, a single battalion, would seldom be ordered to attack by itself. But it would be taking part in a wider operation, with other battalions on its flanks.

I laid it down that we would train whenever possible when we were in a reserve position; training would start by noon on the second day.

We concentrated on fire and movement as we had plenty of small arms ammunition for our brens and rifles. We used it. Also our men dug slit trenches and were bombarded with 3 in mortar bombs directed to fall at a safe distance, but explosive charges were laid near by by the Pioneer to simulate close fire. Besides instilling into the men the art of self-preservation, this process would also lessen the fear element of bombardment when in actual battle. As it turned out, we never had an accident. I emphasized the value of sleep before a battle and ordered the Regimental Police to enforce it (battles are often fought by tired men). I arranged with my excellent Doctor Dick Williams that battle exhaustion cases would be sent to him at the Transport lines and treated there, and not be evacuated to hospitals. Given sleeping pills they in most cases rejoined their Companies in a few days time.

We held a guest night to welcome the officers and the Brigadier came and it was by no means a wake. Parties of all ranks went on brief pleasure trips to Bayeux and some saw George Formby's ENSA show. With the infusion of new blood, the battalion was soon judged to be in a fit state to carry out a reserve role in a forward area, holding the northern slopes of Hill 112.

While still in our convalescent stage, ours was a counter-attack role, should the Germans move back to the hill or retake Fontaine. Supporting us was a squadron of tanks.

A curious phase at this stage of the war was the way the tanks, in compact squadrons, were placed closely behind the leading infantry, where they took the brunt of the mortar fire. In our case, there was sound reason for having them well forward and in front of the River Odon, otherwise their deployment in action would have been slow.

Carefully written orders had been issued by the adjutant Bill Gorman concerning the take over of what as to be our position on Hill 112 on the northern slope. One of my first rulings as CO was that nothing was to be left to chance or memory in this first operation of the newly reformed battalion. Later we relied mainly on verbal orders except for a few confirming notes. Today I have reason to believe that there is too much bunf in the Army. The relief was carried out smoothly, although hampered from time to time by enemy mortaring and considerable air attacks in the Mouen area.

From our forward command post, we had watched anxiously as the great red, gold and black bomb bursts added to the lustre of the starlit sky, and said a quiet prayer that the column would come through untouched. We began to breathe easier as a new concoction of sounds began to infiltrate our ears, the steady rattle and creak of equipment and picks and shovels on the moving men as the rifle companies arrived in the field around the command post. But the bombing had taken its toll. We later learnt that one man had been killed and nine wounded.

After this loss we started a system of moving 20 yards between men when marching to or from the front within enemy mortar or close artillery range to prevent the knocking out of whole section or platoon from enemy fire. The system worked very well.

We spent the next four days in this position planning and practising our counter attack role. I worked out the details with the tank commander under the belly of one of his tanks . . . a rather ingenious form of dug-out. Day and night we rehearsed; standing patrols were set up and changed frequently around the tanks, and patrols were sent out during darkness to contact neighbouring units.

All this activity was carried out under spasmodic enemy fire, and it was of great value in gradually acclimatising the new men and restoring the confidence of the old, some of whom were still shaken by the terrible ordeal on Hill 112, but very few went sick.

On the morning of July 21, a heavy downpour filled our slit trenches . . . dampening our spirits. Part of the battalion moved a few hundred yards to the left into some houses to dry off.

Orders came in the afternoon to relieve 7 Somerset's near the top of the hill. We began our move in single file up the long, reverse slope under cover of darkness. But the Germans were not unaware of our activity; streams of coloured traces whipped over our heads; hostile shells and mortar bombs fell to our left in cluttering spurts of light, to which our guns answered noisily. One shell, swishing overhead with an ominous rush, fell short and wounded a Somerset man.

The relief was complete in the half light of early morning. Our position was in the trampled corn, just below the crest of the hill 112. The companies were within hailing distance of each other, and the foxholes of the platoons within a stone's throw of the next one.

As dawn broke, I visited each company, expressing my satisfaction at the quietness and discipline with which the operation had been carried out. Enemy snipers became a problem during the morning, wounding one of our men. Our own marksmen headed Sgt Long a man of skill and great courage retaliated with effect. About midday, we learnt that 5DCLI were to support 1 Worcester's in a night attack. They were to go for the left, shoulder of Hill 112, while we were to launch a diversionary attack on the right.

Here was an opportunity to use the Scout Platoon.

CHAPTER FOUR

Two Rivers

For this task, the Platoon would be supported by A Coy and backed up by our three inch mortars. Zero hour. As the Worcester's went in, we launched our diversionary attack. Verey lights and star shells illuminated the dark night, and we could hear the staccato bark of the enemy tank machine guns. Tracer bullets criss crossed the night sky, and our positions came under mortar fire.

Dawn brought the depressing news that the attack had failed. But then one glimmer of hope was a report that Major Peter Weston and a handful of Worcester's had made it to their objectives. I ordered Major Colwell with the D Company to move forward and try and contact Peter Weston's men. Colwell who had only just joined us, in making his recce stood up boldly and was shot through the head, he died next to me in the command post a tragedy.

Weston had indeed succeeded to reaching his objection. His grave, and that of his CSM were later discovered at the top of the hill. The news was a blow to me. I had known Peter well during my time with the Worcester's. I can visualise still this tall, athletic man uttering his favourite command: "Don't flap!" A fine Englishman, indeed.

We avenged Colwell's death with a vow to eliminate the enemy snipers in the wooded area around the hill. All Bren guns in the forward area were used to pour withering fire into the trees and hedges from where they were operating. In a short time, we were troubled no further.

For us, it was becoming an artillery and mortar and snipers war. Our gunnery policy was to answer every German shell or mortar with a threefold reply. Shelling reports from the forward companies were acted upon immediately, enemy positions were located by spotters creeping through the corn. Sergeant Long our sniper NCO excelled at this work.

The night of July 25 brought us more tragedy. Intensive

enemy mortar concentration on the command post area killed Captain F.P. Marrian newly out from the Staff College at Camberley and wounded four other ranks. The loss of this brilliant staff-trained officer was keenly felt by all. In his brief time with the battalion he had commanded Support Company with notable success. A misty dawn brought a surprise 'bag' for our look outs in the forward positions. There, just a couple of hundred yards ahead, were three dozen Germans on drill parade! Word was sent back to Battalion HQ, and Captain Gorman, breakfasting on the usual sausage and biscuit, passed the message on to the gunnery officer.

Disappointment was felt when the German NCO dismissed the parade. But he obviously was not satisfied, and ordered them to fall in again. They were finally dismissed by command of the Royal Artillery.

No battalion could have been better served by a battery commander than we were by Major Tom Brewis. Tom of 173 Battery, 179 Fd Regt, RA, was always at my elbow when needed. If he and his wireless sets were not in a slit trench a few yards away, then I knew I could find him in the comparative luxury of a cellar or room nearby, if the command post was sited in a building. On Hill 112, his dug out was joined to mine by a shallow communication trench hacked out of the hard earth. A regular early morning visitor at this time was the brigadier. He would visit us about 7 am each day, and, sitting on top of the communication trench, would discuss with us the happenings of the night before and the prospect of the day to come. From his humour and infectious optimism and confidence, I always felt that, like us, he always had a drop of calvados in his mug of tea! To start with he had rather a difficult time with our General but later was to prove himself as the best of three infantry Brigadiers who were all good men.

Peter Essame was a veteran of 1914-18, and always chose this time for his visit because he knew that the Germans, creatures of habit that they were, could be having breakfast and things would be quiet.

Finally, we were relieved by a battalion of the Monmouthshire Regt, but not before a party of Pioneer Platoon had crept out into no-mans-land during darkness and erected a small sign inscribed "Cornwall Hill, 1944". The battalion had, indeed, left its mark.

Before us stretched three glorious, carefree days of rest. The sheer bliss of a bath, the luxury of clean underwear. Parties of all ranks went to Bayeux and I was with two of my officers and dined with a French family in the town of Bayeux. There were ENSA and cinema shows. A small party of nurses visited the battalion, and were entertained in the HQ mess. Officers paid courtesy visits to other battalions. The war could have been a million miles away, but on the night of July 29 came orders that 43 Division was to move to the Caumont area to take over from an American Division.

Montgomery was skilfully regrouping his forces to knock out the pivots of which Hitler was trying to stabilise his army, and increasing the striking force available to the US 1st Army, which had started its brilliant advance. Avaranches fell on July 30. The enemy were trying desperately to consolidate their position on the hinges of Caumont, on the River Orne, and on the high ground between Caen and Falaise, which included Mount Pincon, the highest point in Normandy and a pivotal position.

The 2nd British Army intended to prevent this by knocking out these key points in succession, from east to west, and the 1st Canadian Army was to advance on Failaise from Caen.

The trap was being set for the destruction of the greater part of the Germany army in France.

The men of the 5DCLI moved in two columns, the rifle companies on foot along the rough, dusty country roads and the motor transport by a longer but better route. I spoke to every platoon, telling the men that the next battle would be the decisive one in the campaign.

By late afternoon, the Brigade was assembled in the La Poumiere area, near Caumont. The countryside, typical Normandy bocage, appeared deceptively green and peaceful, though to our now acclimatised eyes it had that buttoned-up look of enemy territory. We were to find also that it concealed a hidden menace of a thick belt of mines at the foot of the high ground that 130 Brigade had recently taken over from the Americans.

During the night, the brigade assembly area came under air attack, and anti personnel bombs cost us a few casualties. Most of the next day was spent by 130 Brigade in breaching the minefield and eliminating the enemy defences, a slow process.

Then 214 Brigade, led by tanks and the 1st Worcester's, moved forward rapidly to Canteloup, brushing aside enemy resistance. We, being in brigade reserve, were the last to leave.

On foot and mounted on carriers, anti-tank guns and bicycles, the men of 5DCLI moved forward in fading light. As we passed the burning houses, the noise of battle could be heard ahead. Le Cahagnes, a big village on the road, had suffered badly and was still burning fiercely as we filed through it.

On reaching our reserve position in the Canteloup area, shell scrapes were dug and the men, almost asleep on their feet, fell into them.

In between helping mop up pockets of enemy resistance and eliminating troublesome snipers, I re-emphasized our attack doctrine, it was based on the principle of the minimum troops being used to lead an attack and the maximum being held in reserve for manoeuvre. Generally, in a platoon attack, there would be one section up, with the remainder moving in depth over 300 yards behind in open country but close together in wooded terrain. In the Normandy bocage, the leading section worked in pairs to sweep as much open ground as possible.

In company attack, the formation was again generally to be one platoon up and two back. The opening bid in a battalion attack would be one company forward with another in immediate support as moppers-up. The rest of the men two companies, would be held in reserve for manoeuvre.

These tactics were based on the fact that in the battalion, at company and platoon level, one seldom knew with any reasonable degree of accuracy the enemy's exact position. Great depth and the maximum volume of firepower was emphasised for all types of attack.

On August 2, elements of the 43rd Division passed through in its advance to take Mount Pincon. The situation seemed confused. No one could define clearly what our next role would be.

While all ranks of 5DCLI slept during an organised rest period, sleep in war is a most valuable asset and when we could we had enforced rest periods otherwise restless men would keep others awake, I, with my intelligence officer, Captain David Willcocks, went forward on a reconnaissance of the high ground around Jurques, with the idea of acquainting ourselves with the general situation and lay out of the country.

Moving into battle at Mon Le Plessis. Myself and David Willcocks, he is wearing a helmet

The Division itself had captured Jurques but we had suffered considerably in the process. The price our comrades had paid was evident from the crumpled bodies of Wyvern badged soldiers, peaceful in death that lay scattered over a wide area One of our battalions were reported to be on the lower slopes of the Bois de Homme ridge. I contacted the CO who I knew. He was exhausted and he looked to me as if he had little or no sleep for several days. He had lost touch with the enemy and could not tell me where they were, to my great disappointment.

I went back eight miles to the Brigadiers Order Group at La Cahagnes. We received our marching orders: we were to advance guard to the brigade and move forward to make contact with the enemy, who were thought to have fallen back to Mount Pincon the highest hill in Normandy and a pivotal position for the Germans. The carrier platoon moved off about midnight, led by Captain Holland, a debonair figure, but I wished him good fortune. He omitted to tell me that August 3 was his birthday. They were headed for the ridge of high ground the Bois de Homme, that later was to become known as "Tiger Hill" some two miles south of Jurques.

I followed closely in my jeep as they moved through the little village, forlorn and devastated in the moonlight. Detours had to be made round shell craters; here and there a house still burned; knocked out Sherman tank wallowed at the bottom of a large shell, like some crippled, stranded monster. Except for the occasional speculative shell or mortar bomb all was quiet. But as the leading carrier left the village the road improved as it ran downhill to a small bridge about a mile ahead.

Just as the leading carrier past the bridge, a Spandau machine gun opened up. The tracer bullets fired from a great range, swept harmlessly over head, but enough to tell us that the enemy were waiting. Like a large caterpillar in the moonlight, the seven carrier crossed the bridge and crept warily up the high banked road towards the ridge. The spandau had ceased firing and the only noise was the roar of the carriers as they dropped into bottom gear to tackle the incline.

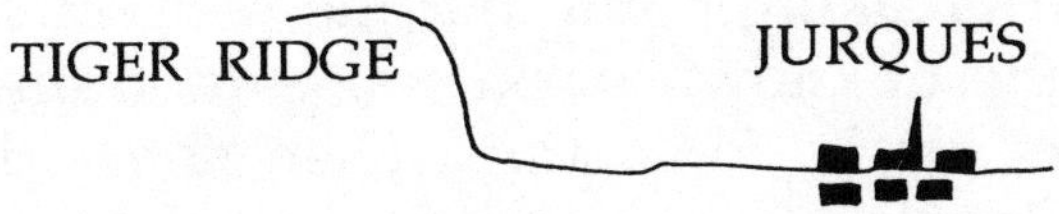

JURQUES 3RD AUGUST 1944

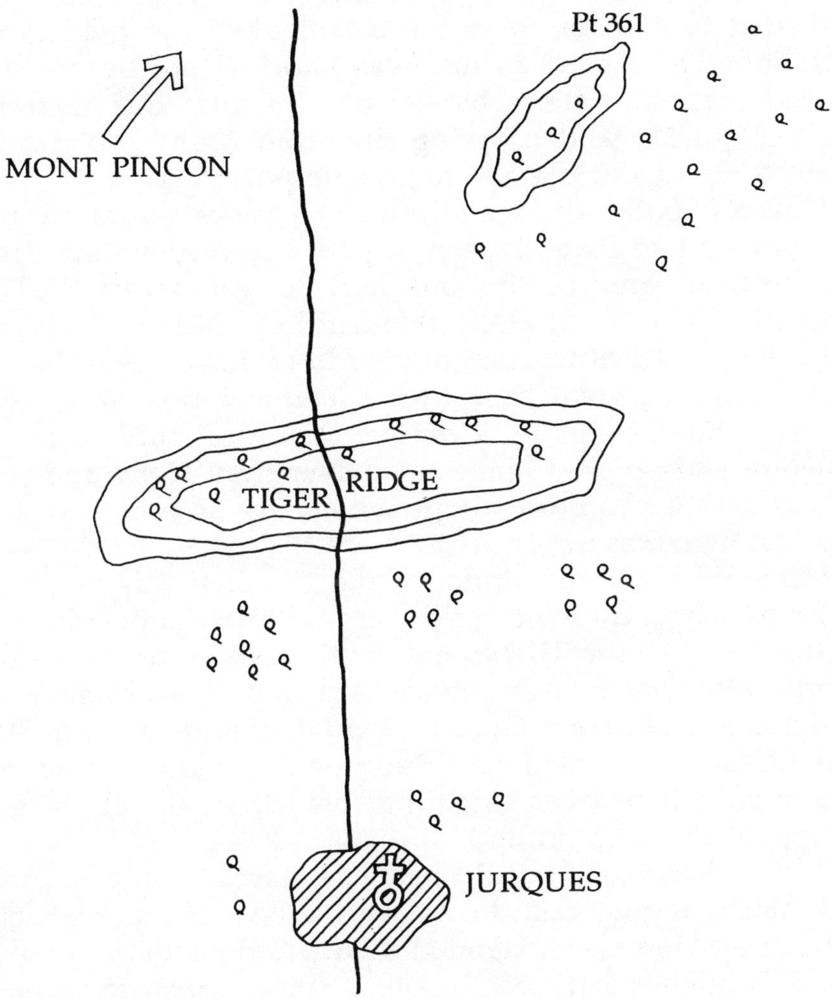

Halfway up the column stopped to listen. Silence. It was uncanny. Holland and the crew of the leading carrier went forward 50 yards to check for mines, but the road appeared to be clear.

Nerves were at breaking point, but the platoon continued on its way into the unknown darkness, guns trained ahead and to the flanks ready for action. Then some time after midnight, as the leading carrier approached the brow of the hill, all hell broke loose as Spandaus and Tank guns opened up fire at close range, firing straight down the hill at the column. Flares also went up. The first carrier slewed round and tried to bolt for cover but a tank shell put paid to this ambition. The second in line was knocked out by grenades lobbed from the steep banks, but by now our men had reacted quickly and covering fire from Brens and mortars enabled the carrier platoon to take up positions.

Holland coolly set us a string of 75 mines across the road covered by two Piats, he sent a patrol to retrieve the Brens, ammunition and equipment and to get away the two wounded men. I told Holly (Holland) to hold on at all costs until the arrival of C Company, who by now would be well on their way. I went back in my Jeep and met Major Ruck Keene, the Company Commander and told him the situation and ordered him to take over from Holly and see if he could find out more about the enemy. It was now 4 am and first light was not far away.

Meanwhile, the remainder of the battalion was beginning to arrive after a difficult march because of the congested state of the road as the Divisional Artillery was on the move. Shortly after dawn, they and a Squadron of Sherman Tanks of the 4/7th Dragoon Guards, the latter under Major Steve Jenkins had assembled near Jurques . . . the morning mist and thick belt of trees shielding them from the sharp eyed enemy on the high ground.

In the distance, we could hear the staccato bark of enemy tank machine guns and the answering beat of our Bren guns as Ruck Keene's men extended their positions to the flanks.

The Brigadier arrived at about 6 am and instructed me to clear the high ground. The heat was on; the Americans had begun their great breakthrough in the west and the 15th Scottish Division and the Guards Armoured Division, were making on our right good progress and our Division had to conform. We needed to secure the ridge urgently to protect the flank of our Division during its intended advance to knock out the pivot Mount Pincon, which it was believed the enemy would hold strongly. The time factor precluded out any hopes of outflanking the enemy with a wide turning movement and in any case the German doctrine on defence was to try and hold on a broad front . . . but I did not like the idea of a frontal head on attack . . . it looked a formidable position held by tanks and infantry but in what strength and when we could not tell we were to gather bitter fruit because of the failure of the forward battalion to keep touch with the enemy. We were given only two hours to prepare for our attack. I asked for more but it was not granted, but I added 15 minutes. I knew that there were many examples in World War 1 of mist or fog covering the attackers notably the Germans in March 1918 in their great offensive.

I hoped to take advantage of the mist to close with the enemy and had to plan only from the map, but the mist suddenly dissolved and the sun came out and it was a cloudless day which precluded the effective use of smoke, as it would spiral.

C Company would be our spearhead but the tanks would move with D Company just behind the leading Company, thus C I hoped would make the enemy tanks draw their fire and our Shermans could take them on; the other two companies were held back in reserve. I stressed depth in my orders. The attack was to be supported by two Artillery Field Regt firing a barrage as we could not concentrate our fire as we had not been able to locate the enemy. Mortars and Machine guns were to cover the flanks. I asked the Brigadier for the rocket firing Typhoons to deal with the tanks. But Divisional Headquarters could not get them for us, no doubt they were being used on what was considered more important targets.

As the mist began to clear, the company commanders

could see enough to plan their respective tactics. I advised Ruck Keene to keep clear of the road and to use a slight right hook that would enable him to use what little cover there was, also to use his two inch mortars to cover his right flank with smoke, hopefully.

They went in at 8.15 am covered by the artillery barrage, the leading platoons of C Company sweeping all before then in a workmanlike manner Lieut F.W. Dureden relates: "moving close to our bursting shells 'Suddenly' we saw the enemy in their slit trenches. We charged forward, firing from the hip. We killed several of them. The rest got up and ran away. We hit a number of them."

The Germans put down a concentration of mortar defensive fire on left side of the road, but it took some time for their mortar teams to discover the exact direction of our thrust. Durden's platoon began to move on, when cleverly concealed enemy tanks started to fire at them. The platoon hit the ground and we engaged them with small arms fire and two inch mortars "we could not get close enough to engage them with our Piats".

While the defenders were thus engaged, the rest of the company were able to cross the road, and Lieut Welch's platoon reached the ring contour which was their objective.

But things were getting too hot for Durden and his men. Much reduced by casualties, they retreated to the cover of a small hump about 100 yards away.

Meanwhile, Lieut R. Prowse, leading platoon D Company, tried to get his men across the road to support the attackers with small arms fire, but the tank fire was deadly. Several soldiers were killed in the attempt and others wounded. Some of the fearsome Tigers were stationary spiting death from their well concealed lairs, while others lumbered about more ominously.

Major Fry, D Coy, decided to move his men and the survivors of Durden's depleted platoon into wooded country on the left of the road. Related Durden: "This position was no better than the open, gorse-covered hill, as the 88 shells and mortar bombs burst in the trees." Casualties began to mount. With the wireless set out of order, Major Fry sent me back to the command post to report the situation."

It was a bleak picture that unfolded for the lieutenant as he made his way back; a few stragglers and walking wounded trudging their dejected way down the hill, past the shattered hulks of two British tanks. From the command post near the church, I had watched from the church steeple the early stages of the attack go according to plan. I saw C Coy clear the top of the ridge and a wireless report came in to say they were successfully dealing with the enemy infantry.

But then came the news of serious opposition from the Tigers. We saw one of our tanks explode in a column of smoke and flame, bringing to a halt its armoured comrades on the road leading up to the ridge.

The enemy mortar fire was a terrible and frightening sight as it crept its sinister way forward like some evil, gigantic black beast from the bottom of the lovely green valley, with its trees and grass reflecting the sunlight, upwards towards our command post until the bombs were exploding around us.

Our tanks made a further effort to get to grips with the enemy, but another was knocked out as it attempted to get over the crest line. We had tried bombarding the German Tanks with our 25 pounders, but they proved ineffectual. So we decided to use our medium artillery, which meant pulling back the infantry from the danger zone. But by this time, the men were so mixed up near the enemy. We did not fully realise this back at the command post, and on the order to fall back about 500 yards, some of them came right back beyond the foot of the hill, where they were later collected and reformed. I was worried that there might be a repeat of the disorderly retreat from Hill 112.

I decided to send in the reserves. Moving forward under shellfire with A Coy and a platoon of sappers, I came across a despondent group of company and platoon officers huddled in a roadside farmhouse who broke to me the gloomy news of the heavy casualties suffered by the two leading companies.

I berated them for leaving their men in a crisis without their platoon commanders and sent them back to their companies, but first of all getting their information.

Meanwhile, fire was continuing to rain down on us from the top of the ridge. We realised that while we could not get our tanks to the top any further assault by the infantry would be doomed to failure. About this time, the brigadier arrived to assess the situation and decided to use the Worcester in a right hook flank attack.

We had come up against a brick wall. After the losses on Hill 112 we could not afford another disaster. We had to approach the problem by more devious means. If we could get a few men up round the right and locate his flank behind the enemy.

I called in Sgt Long, our sniper expert who could have taught Davy Crockett a thing or two in fieldcraft. He required only two men, snipers Chapman and Nichols.

Long recalled, "The sun was streaming down when we started off, and it was no easy job to crawl for the best part of a mile along hedgerows and ditches to avoid being spotted. But we kept going and gradually got nearer the top of the hill." About 200 yards from the summit, the trio stuck lucky, coming across a small gully that ran over the top of the hill. Both sides were covered in tall, protective fern. In a short time, the patrol had reached its objective and was looking down on the enemy from behind.

"Although the fern had helped us get over the top of the hill, it now became a hindrance, because we could not see a thing that was near enough for us to take a shot at," said Sgt Long. But 400 yards ahead was a house surrounded by bushes. It was derelict. Peering through the gaps left by missing tiles, Long found the perfect observation post.

It was not long before the three snipers saw a group of five Germans emerge from their dug out about 200 yards away.

Said Long, "They started to set up a mortar as if they were playing in their own backyards. On the word of 'fire' from me, the volley went forth. "Through our sights, we could see only two men left standing and they soon dived for cover".

The light was beginning to fade, and Long decided that contact had to be established with the battalion. Leaving Chapman and Nichols in the house, he crept back through the ferns to battalion HQ. I sent him back with a wireless set so as to keep us at the command post informed of developments on the enemy side of the hill.

Now in contact with the battalion, Long and his companions resumed their lonely vigil. "Early next morning we snatch every opportunity to make those Germans feel our ammunition," said the sergeant. "It was amusing to watch the look of bewilderment on their faces when they realised they were being sniped at from behind their own lines.

"Every now and then, we were fortunate enough to bowl over one or two and their number was gradually dwindling. Even so, I cannot understand how they failed to give the house we were in the once over to make sure it was not the hide-out of a sniper or two."

But the house remained immune and Long, Chapman and Nichols remained masters of all they surveyed. "It gave you the feeling you were pinching sweets from children," confessed Long.

At about the same time as Long set out on his mission our Signal Officer Captain Max Stock, who was a fluent French speaker came to me and said that their was a Frenchman M. Solier, a refugee from Paris staying in a farm, who had offered to help us. And as it was essential to try out where the enemy right flank was, we concocted a plan. Max and M. Solier were to become two men out ferreting and disguised with a bag of ferrets. They were moving down the ditch, when suddenly they saw a pair of substantial jackboots. They belonged to a large German Sergeant Major, who was in an angry mood. They quickly realised that he was lost. Discretion being the better part of valour, they decided to lure him back to the British lines by guile.

Solier told him there was a wounded German at his farm who needed help. The man failed to rise to the bait, until Solier told him his wife was cooking a good meal. Whereupon, the German nobly agreed to accompany them on a mission of mercy.

Halfway back, the soldier halted, to answer a call of nature. Handing Stock his pistol, he went about his business. There was the enemy literally with his trousers down, but still it was not the opportune moment, Max decided. He politely handed the gun back, because they might meet an enemy patrol.

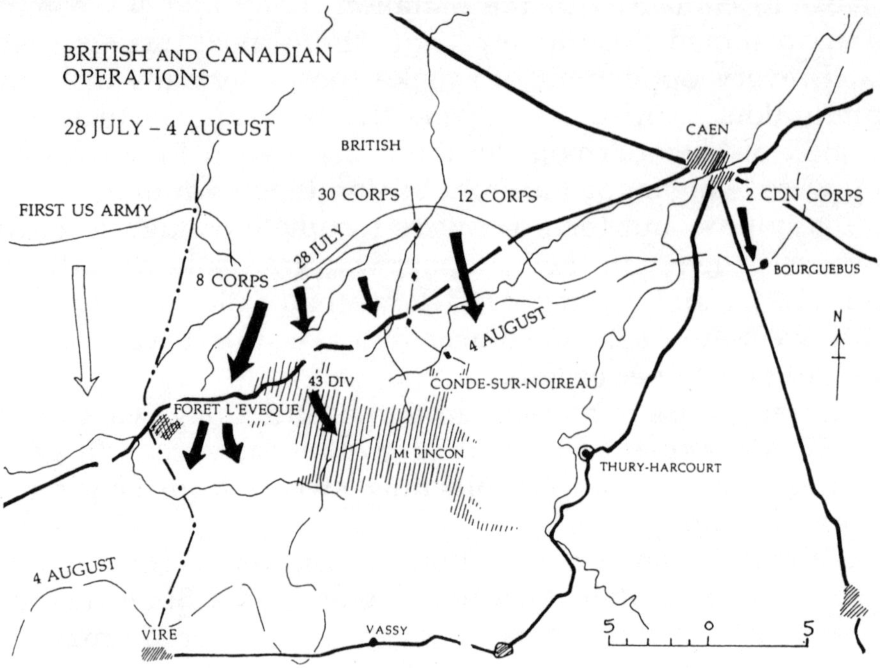

THE BREAKOUT

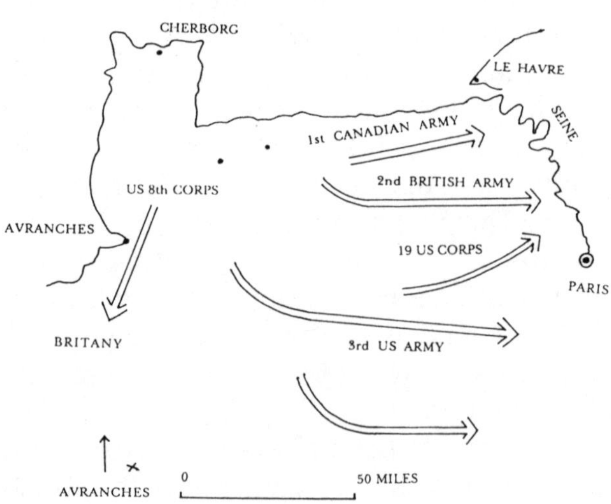

The sergeant major was made welcome by Solier's wife, who had been alerted and with clean napkins tucked in his collar, he sat down to enjoy the French hospitality. The noise of a motorcycle interrupted the diners, and, making his apologies Stock left the room. It was a despatch rider with the officer's revolver. Returning calmly to the room, Max sat down, levelled the pistol at the guest and said: "Hands up". The astonished German complied.

Much valuable information was learned from the sergeant major, including the fact that the enemy's main body had fallen back several miles. It was an example of just how useful such a ferreting expedition can be in war. And it earned Max Stock the Military Cross and M. Solier the Kings Medal for Courage in the Cause of Freedom.

It could be said that this was a misuse of a Signals Officer, and should not have been risked on the other hand we have in Sgt Frank Grigg an efficient signals sergeant, a splendid and most amusing man – who from time to time entertained us with George Robie Patter and song. It was he who in the past war years, with two other CSM B. Tremain and CQMS Cedric Ivens, who have worked splendidly to hold the 'Old Comrades Association' of the 5th together. The average attendance at the Reunion Dinner in Cornwall being over 100 men, some coming from all parts of Britain many with their wives. What a wonderful spirit after 45 years.

Long came on the radio and told us that the enemy were pulling out taking their wounded with them in trucks.

Helped by the Worcestershire flanking hook (somewhat delayed because the leading company lost it's way in the woods) Tiger Hill was at last being tamed. Early that morning with speed we occupied the ridge – dug in and then the Reconnaissance Regiment past through.

The final irony was that the Typhoons that I had requested before the 'action' now struck, leaving two of our men wounded.

The RAF later sent a message of apology. Though the ridge was in our hands, but again the 5th DCLI had suffered another blooding; this time we had 20 dead and 69 wounded and 10 missing. Three of our carriers had been destroyed and the 4/7th Dragoon Guards had lost two tanks. We had been up against a strong rear guard of 10 tanks one rifle company and mortar teams, and our old enemy 10 SS Panzer Division. We counted 30 dead Panzer Grenadiers and there must have been more wounded who had got away. Depth, in the attack undoubtably saved a calamity. We were handicapped as we did not know the 4/7 Dragoon Guards and therefore team work was lacking. It might be said that after we had contacted the enemy the Brigadier should have told us just to contain the enemy only whilst he put in a hook with the Worcestershire's.

Of course, there was great pressure on the Brigadier from the Division to attack at once. Later, we were able to develop a great team spirit with the 4/7th Dragoon Guards and with 13/18th Hussars and Sherwood Rangers of the 8th Armoured Brigade commanded by that excellent soldier Brigadier Prior Palmer.

In our future operations, we nearly had a least one squadron of the Brigade working with us and we reckoned that they were second to none. At Jurques we lost only one officer a most gallant subaltern the son of a most distinguished General-Tuker, this very brave young man had in spite of my warning that no replenishment of ammunition was to be attempted till we were secure on the top of the ridge, had gallantly rushed forward in his ammunition carrier to be killed by an enemy tank. A very sad loss but the only officer casualty, which illustrated the quality of our NCOs. Moving forward towards Mont Pincon, we heard the news that the 5th Wiltshire's had met very strong resistance from the enemy in carefully concealed positions behind a fast flowing stream at the foot of the feature and their Colonel Jackie Pearson, with a red rose in his cap had gone gallantly forward to commemorate the battle of Minden to encourage his men, had been killed shot through the heart by a sniper, who in turn was quickly dealt with but the enemy had by the bravery and hard fighting of the Wiltshire's been forced to disclose his defences. Then the Somerset's battalion came into action.

Covered by the devastating fire of our artillery Lt Colonel Lipscombe 4th Somerset's made progress and getting a footing on the lower slopes in spite of considerable mortar fire. Then with great boldness a squadron of 13/18 Hussars under Denny, negotiating a mine field and most difficult terrain, reached the crest of Mont Pincon, with seven Sherman Tanks. Lipscombe an excellent commander, saw them against the skyline. Quickly appreciating the situation, got his exhausted men to go forward, the heat was sweltering, they reached the Shermans and dug in on the stony ground, Brigadier Mole quickly reinforced them with elements of 4th Wiltshire's under Lt Colonel Luce. In a mist that morning a strong German counter attack went astray. This great bastion of a hill had fallen to the skill and bravery and co-operation of all arms, but above all to the endurance, fighting spirit and sacrifice of the West Country men, the infantry and the initiative of Denny.

Meanwhile we were resting in reserve about four miles from Mont Pincon, the red Normandy earth seemed to dance under a glittering sun. We sent out the Scout Platoon and the Carrier Platoon in the general direction of Le Plessis Grimault and to the west, to see if they could locate the enemy, without much success, though they surprised a party of Germans sun bathing near a farm a strange lapse of discipline and shot them up inflicting casualties. Late on the afternoon of the 7th August, Brigadier Peter Essame arrived and said, "George, I want you to capture Le Plessis Grimault, a village that lay at the foot of Mont Pincon." He said that it was an important communication centre. This accomplished, it would open the road to Aumay-sur-Odon and Conde-sur-Noireau, the proposed axis of the 7th Armoured Divisions thrust to the south. I was to come with him on a recce. I realised that it would soon be dark and my company and Platoon commanders would not be able to see the ground, but I could make sure that at least A Company's commander would, so I took with me Major Harry Parker and his platoon commanders. There was considerable shelling as in our Jeeps we reached the foothills and near the top of Mont Pincon there was a direct hit on a Sherman

Tank and it went up with a horrible vivid whoof. Crawling into the top, we could just see the red roof tops of Le Plessis Grimault. The Brigadier David Willcocks Harry Parker and I crawled forward.

MATADOR

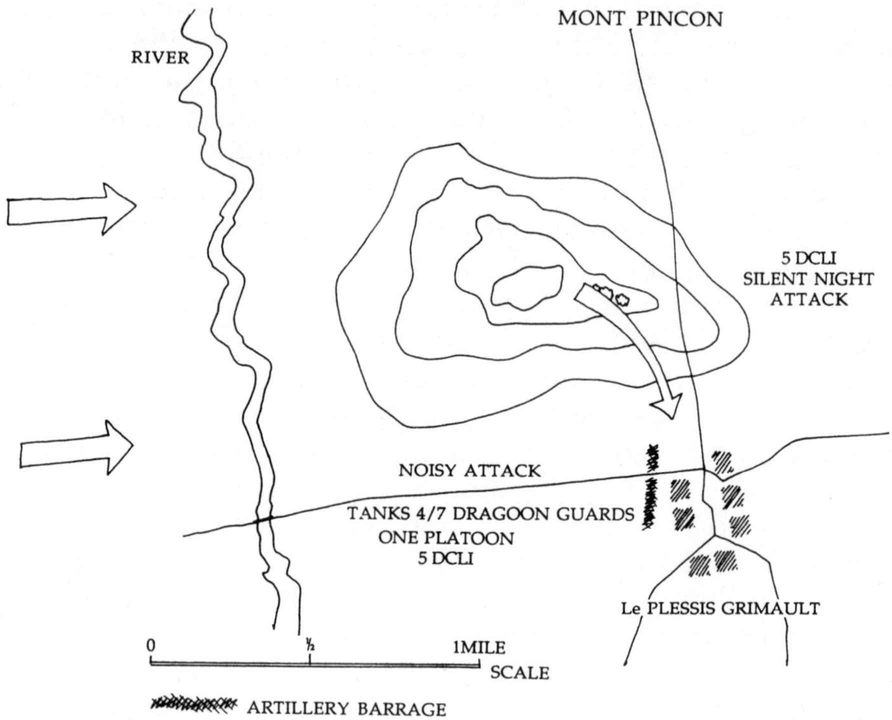

I was determined that there was not going to be a repeat of the Jurques type of frontal attack and that we would seek to surprise the enemy. He, we assumed, would try and hold the village in strength. Though as was often the case, we had no information about his whereabouts. The essence of infantry tactics could be likened to a policeman tackling a desperate man in a dark room – one had to find him first with one hand before hitting him with a baton. The plan was for B Squadron 4/7th Dragoon Guards less one Troop to act as noisy decoy, on the axis of the road west of the village and to the right of the hill, to draw the enemy fire. They were to be covered by a block barrage consisting of the fire of three Field Regiments and one Median Regiment over 90 pieces of artillery, our mortars and machine guns were to cover the right flank, if any Germans with anti tank weapons were left, they would be lucky men. But, to take care of this possibility, I allotted Steve Jenkins the tank squadron commander, on rifle platoon, he had asked me for a rifle company I refused as indirect artillery and mortar fire would be unlikely to knock his tanks out, but, infantry in company strength would get a lot of casualties. The Brigadier having accepted my plan, departed, to make sure of the artillery support. I gave Parker his orders to attack and capture the village and then went back to meet the battalion, which had reached an assembly area in the foothills.

I gave out my orders to the company commanders, Tom Brewis my Gunner, and two specialist officers. A Company was to be the assault company, my little command group were to move behind the assault company and then D Company in close support, just behind us. C and B Companies were to be held well back in reserve and dig shell scrapes. Nowadays with the great range and accuracy of indirect fire it is essential that Infantry reserves dig in even if only shell scrapes. The Infantry's part of the attack was to be a silent one, as the light began to fade we moved over the crest and down hill towards Le Plessis shielded to some extent by the high bracken and a few birch trees and the poor light, the enemy failed to see us. Meanwhile, the Divisional Artillery had opened fire and with a thunderous crash supplemented by the battalions three inch mortars firing to the right flank of the barrage.

Behind this moving barrage of flying steel, smoke an dust moved the tanks, with Welch's platoon of C Company well dispersed amongst the armour, all moving on the axis of the road from La Varinere; getting close to the village the tanks opened fire with their BESA machine guns. It was now dark. Suddenly, there was a deafening explosion as an enemy ammunition store exploded in a fury of gold and red flame. This magnificent bonfire acted as a beacon for the attack. Light signals from the village were going up and the night was alight with streams of tracer bullets. Heavy mortar fire was coming down on the tanks our plan was working, and the pressure on me seemed to ease. I went forward down the hill following A Company, when suddenly I saw a figure. He was a young corporal from 'A'. He said that he had lost his way which I doubted so I said come with me and on we went.

Harry Parker and his men had moved silently unobserved, to the northern edge of the village. It was whilst waiting for the barrage to lift that the battalion won an unexpected bonus. Harry and his men heard the movement of tank tracks, only a very short distance away sending for a Piat, he was annoyed to find that the man had no bombs, but Harry not to be out done, brought a two inch mortar into action, this speculative effort brought an instant result. There was a tremendous roar and an explosion. As the leading Section rushed forward they saw an enemy tank crew running away from it and another large tank departing in haste. They found that the mortar bomb had hit an ammunition lorry replenishing the tanks. The captured tank was a Royal Tiger of 62 tons. It was the first of this type of tank to fall into British hands. This little epic must have shaken enemy moral in the village.

Quickly following up, Harry launched his company. With an encircling attack one platoon attacking the east side and one platoon attacking the west side, whilst the third platoon with him attacked down the centre of the village down the main street. It was close quarter work and a lot of grenades were used after over an hours fighting the defence collapsed. Harry described it as a sweet battle, he was a warrior. I will never forget the sight of enemy prisoners being marched down the village street lit by the glow of burning houses. German dead and wounded lay scattered about, the village had been held by two rifle companies. We captured 125 of them and our losses were two men killed, one missing and five wounded. Truly a tactical surprise in which the armour with fortitude and great co-operation played its part – no tanks of ours were knocked out.

The 62 Ton Royal Tiger Tank captured by 'A' Company in the Le Plessis Grimault battle 8th August

German Prisoners captured by the Battalion in Normandy

Afterwards I called it "Operation Matador", the tanks being the cloak and the Infantry the sword. And under Harry a sharp sword it was. The two master principles of war surprise and concentration were used to great affect. If things had not worked out to plan I had the flexibility for the use of a strong reserve. Shortly before dawn avenging German artillery and mortar fire brought roofs and walls crashing round us and we had a few men wounded including Harry but fortunately only slightly. Two minor counter attacks were easily beaten off, a German Officer prisoner was brought to me, he gave me the Hitler salute. To say the least of it I was not pleased. Then I heard from my command post the roar of approaching tanks. Soon, we would be a back area. Or so I thought.

The leading troop commander came in to report to me. Perhaps unfortunately at that moment Sgt Thorpe, my intelligence sergeant, came into the command post with the news that there were three Tiger Tanks outside the village. The young officers very ears seemed to flap. The immediate effect was that his troop of tanks did not move, the squadron did not move. The whole of the 7th Armoured Division stayed just where it was.

Our own tanks 4th/7th Dragoon Guards had been withdrawn to refit and rest. Later a Brigade of the 50 Division was brought up to continue the advance. Perhaps, the momentum of our thrust could have been promptly maintained. If the practice of General Sir Brian Horrocks our wonderful Corps Commander had been followed by a senior officer of the 7th Armoured Division (smelling out the battle as Horrocks called it) our success could have been exploited more quickly. With a good artillery fire plan and our superiority in tank numbers we could have probably swamped the three tigers.

The 7th Armoured Division which had greatly distinguished itself against the Germans and Italians in the deserts of the Middle East and North Africa. Brought back to Britain, it had trained in country completely different than it was to face in the bocage of Normandy. If it had been sent to the West Country where the terrain bears some resemblance to that of Normandy vital security would have been lost.

Heavy losses amongst tank commanders who had to expose themselves, from snipers in the thick country had in general made the Division over cautious, but after Normandy, with a new Divisional Commander they regained their old vigour and dash and again became an elite force. There was a requirement for an SOP (Standing Operational Order) that in a Division or Brigade headquarters a senior commander or senior staff officers should go forward at what is judged a critical time, especially after a successful attack to counter the natural inertia that sets in amongst victorious troops. After a unit has captured a strongly held position and suffered casualties. A sensitive commander is apt to think we have done our stuff and I don't want to risk having more casualties.

With 7th Armoured Division finally on its way to its rendezvous with the Americans, the Cornwall's were to clear pockets of enemy resistance on the left flank of the main axis. The first objective was the village of La Trulandiere, and from there we were to move to the bigger settlement of Culey Le Patry. Major Rucke Keene's company located the main enemy position after passing through La Trulandiere and a quick plan was formulated. While Keene occupied the attention of the German troops holding a long ridge protecting Culey, I took the reserve platoon from C Company to reinforce D and protect the left flank.

D Company advanced in a wide outflanking movement, skilfully avoiding detection by the enemy occupying the high ground north of Culey. It was during this action that we witnessed one of the luckiest escapes of the war! Lieut Prowse, the leading platoon commander, ably backed by his section commanders, quickly and skilfully eliminated machine gun posts set up by the Germans to protect the covered approach to the village.

Prowse suffered the personal trauma of having an anti tank missile pass between his legs. Fortunately, the only wound he suffered was to his dignity, and this gallant officer though badly shaken lived to tell the tale and to be a father.

Meanwhile D Company had come into action on the left.

Now supported by the covering fire of two companies, D Company crossed the road from the north and seized the ridge. The light was failing, and I decided to consolidate and continue the advance on the village next morning. The attack had been carried through like a demonstration at the School of Infantry . . . and this without the use of my crack A Company, which I held in reserve.

By mid August, 1944, the battle of Normandy had reached crisis point. Disregarding the advice of his generals, Hitler ordered that the Panzer divisions be disengaged and reformed outside Mortain, in preparation for an attack outside Avranches, which they did affecting a partial breakthrough of some seven miles but the brave and stubborn resistance of the American 30th Infantry Division near Mortain ruined the enemy plan. But with ideal weather for air operations, then the combined power of the Allied air forces was used to the greatest effect against the enemy ground columns. Against such overwhelming odds, the result was never in doubt. With the bulk of the enemy armour still committed on the extreme east flank, the British Sector the Germans could not afford to yield an inch, and they based their defences on village strongpoints in depth, with tanks or self propelled guns in support and deadly mortars. After clearing up what remained of the enemy defences south and south west of Mount Picon, it was left to 7 Armoured and 50 Divisions to continue the main thrust of the advance towards Conde and the River Noireau.

On the afternoon of August 12, 5DCLI and 7 Somerset Light Infantry were ordered to eliminate what remained of the enemy in the hilly and wooded country around Mont Gaultier and Culey le Patry, down to the River Orne. With 11 Armoured Division placed under his command from first light on August 14, General Brian Horrocks decided to push forward without further ado on the right flank to the road which runs due south from Conde to Flers. To 43 Division fell the task of forcing a crossing of the Noireau east of Conde and then advancing to Athis, two miles beyond. Brigadier Essame briefed us that night, and the battalion was astir early next morning for its move of 25 miles to the south. Battalion and company commanders spent the morning reconnoitring the area generally. Across the River Noireau could be seen the wooded heights, wreathed in a smoky haze from fires started by our artillery fire which continued spasmodically all morning. The enemy, anticipating our next move, kept up intense shelling and mortar fire on the cross roads and approaches to the river. The brigadier briefed us again at 1400 hours, in the big chateau. The brigade was to cross the river and storm the heights on the opposite side.

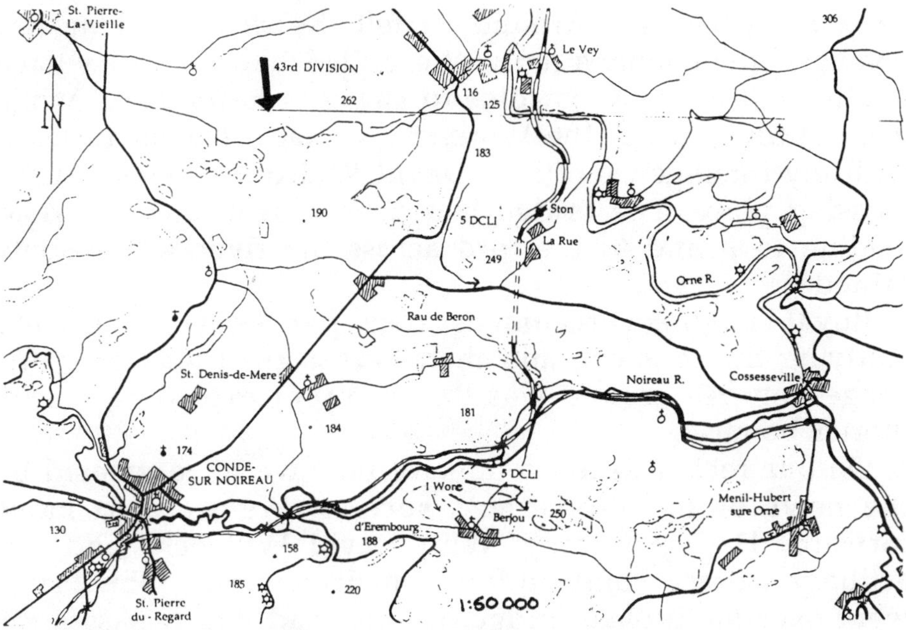

The Worcester's were to take the high ground around Berjou, on the right, and the Somerset's were to concentrate on Le Hamel, to the left. We in 5DCLI were in brigade reserve, to exploit the success of either battalion according to the situation.

H Hour was to be at 6 pm with the attack supported by artillery fire, 4.2 inch mortars, and the machine guns of 8 Middlesex. Meanwhile, I had reached my own conclusions. During an afternoon reconnaissance of the target area, it became apparent to me that, due to the nature of the ground and the probability of bad communications, if we waited back in a central position for news of the success of either one or other of the battalions before moving up, the battalion would never be able to reach the top of the ridge before dark. I decided to follow the Worcester's as closely as possible, banking on their early success.

The battalion moved to an assembly area about three miles from the river. The traffic on the dusty roads was continuous and we were lucky to be able to reach the assembly point in time. We followed the Worcester's along the narrow roads towards Noireau, watching the tall trees that flanked us sway gently in the breeze created by our supporting barrage. Around us fell the shells and mortar bombs of the enemy's reply. We pulled into a small village reminiscent of the Cotswolds to snatch a hasty meal, while waiting for news of the Worcester's attack. I went forward with my intelligence officer, David Willcocks, to seek out a crossing place. The bridge had been blown, and the road leading to it and to the ford across the river was heavily mined.

Royal Engineer reconnaissance parties were already studying the problem, and there was a great deal of traffic congestion. All around was the crump of exploding enemy mortar bombs.

On our return to the command post we were greeted by the news of the Worcester's success. We were to move forward, D Coy leading. With David Willcocks and our artillery battery commander Tom Brewis and John Fry, I went over the broken bridge, up the road which passes the railway station and through the gardens clustered at the foot of the river bridge.

Some 200 yards to the right, the enemy mortar bombs were exploding with deafening roars. We waded across the shallow river and moved into the gloomy wood, still burning in places from the bombardment; the acid smoke caught in our lungs.

Up the steep slope we went, the battalion following. We heard that the Worcester's had taken their objective and had three companies on the top of the Ridge. Later we were to find that this was not so, but they had only got a footing on the Ridge.

We continued our climb, and half an hour late were approaching the top. By this time it was dark and the tracers bullets were penciling the sky with coloured trails. The noisy rattle of enemy's 42 machine guns told us that possession of high ground was still in dispute. Just below the crest of the ridge, where the woods thinned out, I met Captain Doc Watson, the Worcester's right hand company commander I knew him well and he was very glad to see me. From what he told me, and from the constant tearing BRRRRRRRRRP of the German machine guns, it was evident that they were holding the top in some force, two battalions, we found out later. With the bridge across the Noirea destroyed, we had been unable to get our heavy wireless vehicles over, which meant we were without artillery support. I decided to dig in just ahead of the Worcester's and see what the dawn brought. There was no point in risking a night attack as in the dark we could not see the ground to organise a night attack.

With A, B and C Companies, DCLI, forming a solid triangle in front of the Worcester's, it meant that six companies were sited on the edge of the plateau that night, with the enemy only 80 yards away. They harassed us with mortar fire, and losses among the Worcester's began to mount. I made a tour of their companies in an effort to cheer up my former regimental comrades, and to co-ordinate the defensive layout. But there was little for any of us to be happy about. The ground was hard, which made the business of digging in difficult while waiting to ward off an expected attack at the same time. It was a miserably cold night, and we could feel the sweat of our recent exertions drying chillingly on our backs. We had climbed the hill in shirtsleeve order. Then, to add to our troubles my small wireless set, operated by the excellent L/Cpl Williams, went on the blink, no doubt due to the surrounding hills and woods.

This meant we were out of contact with the brigade, so I decided to send back Captain Willcocks to report the situation and to stress the urgency of the early arrival of the long awaited anti-tank guns and the tanks of the Sherwood Rangers, and the artillery battery commander Tom Brewis. Meanwhile, back at the river crossing, the adjutant, Bill Gorman, was having his own problems. It was his job to get the support vehicles and supplies across as quickly as possible and get them up the hill in time for the assault on the ridge. He recalls: "The approach to the cross of the River Noireau was a rough, narrow, winding road which ran down gently through open fields and woodland to a small village on the near bank of the river.

"Here, the railway bridge had been blown by the retreating Germans, and the whole area was heavily mined and over looked by the steep, wooded heights on the opposite side. The crossing of the river was no obstacle to the Infantry, who could scramble over the broken bridge but it was clear that no transport could be got across until a firm crossing site had been made. Not only was it necessary to 'delouse' the road for mines but also to clear a lane through the extensive minefields which protected the likely crossing places.

Said Gorman,

"This proved to be an awkward task, as time was short; night had fallen before the sapper reconnaissance had been completed, and the whole area was constantly shelled and mortared from the prominent heights on the opposite side. But the infantry were across and fighting their way up the ridge. By first light, they would be sorely in need of ammunition, food and their own heavy weapons and tank support and the artillery big wireless set."

So the long night was spent in anxious waiting, in impatient visits to the site to see how the work was progressing, in efforts to obtain and disseminate information over extended distances, and in constant shuffling and reshuffling of the transport priorities as the night progressed and the situation was deemed to require. Mines scattered at random on the verges of the road hindered the slow progress, and the resulting casualties and damaged vehicles necessitated a slow and laborious searching of the whole area. At the level crossing near the river a large truck blew up, blocking the road. The REME breakdown vehicle which came to clear it away suffered a similar fate, increasing the difficulties and causing further delay. Captain Gorman continues: "Nor was the narrow road suitable for heavy traffic. One tank was sufficient to block the road, and as always happens on these occasions, all the transport in the British Army arranged to be present, all the carriers decided to shed their tracks simultaneously, and all the drivers developed a sudden and passionate desire to go in any opposite direction."

The situation was not eased any when, at about midnight, it was decided to pass the Somersets' transport through our crossing place and to give it priority.

This involved more movement in the restricted approaches and a further shuffling of transport in the dark. It was not surprising, therefore, that it was long after first light before the battalion transport and that of our supporting arms, following hard on the heels of the Somerset's and Worcestershire's, was able to cross the river and to make its way slowly towards the companies which were already dug in on the high crests overlooking the river and in close contact with the enemy in the outskirts of Berjou Village.

* * *

On the top of the hill, as the sky became pale in the east, the men of the six companies, weary and chilled from their long night's vigil, crouched in their shallow trenches their hands tense on rifle or Bren apprehensive of what the dawn would bring.

The day started peacefully enough, and I took the opportunity to move along the hedge to get my first clear glimpse of the enemy positions. The main tactical point was a slight bump in the ground on the left of the road. It was held partly by the Worcester's and partly by the Germans.

Neither the anti-tanks guns nor the tanks had yet arrived, but Tom Brewis brought us some comfort in the form of his big artillery wireless set, which put us back in contact with the artillery and brigade headquarters. David Willcocks had arrived back from his night travels with news of Gorman's dauntless efforts to get the guns and tanks across the river and up the main road. We knew the morning lull in enemy hostilities was too good to last, and sure enough the mortar bombs began falling again in black vivid crashed among us. We hugged our shallow scrapes in the ground and prayed to the Almighty. The main target seemed to be the edge of the wood just behind the battalion command post. There was little doubt that Jerry had an observation post on top of the small bump.

While waiting for the armour and the arrival of DCLI's A Coy, still at the bottom of the hill, we decided to try to consolidate our toe-hold on the plateau so that we could deploy them better when they reached us. B Coy was detailed to eliminate the machine gun posts in front of D Coy. They went in under cover of a smoke-screen, and after eliminating two, Machine Gun Posts, but were held up by the withering fire of the MG 42s sited in depth.

The BRRRRRRRRRP of the deadly fusillade came back to us, like the sound of some giant tearing up monstrous playing cards in his powerful hands. It was now the enemy's turn to try to push us back off the ridge. They began with an infantry attack on the left hand company of Worcester's. Major Matthews, their company commander, was badly wounded in the arm. Casualties were mounting among the DCLI and the Worcester's, and a steady stream of men were being evacuated from left to right in front of the wood. The edge of the wood became a death trap. The Germans then attacked on the extreme right of D Coy and succeeded in bringing in range of their small arms the top of the track which led down the hill. Thus, our communication to the rear was cut off. Just in time, came a welcome roar from behind, and the leading tanks appeared, supported by part of A Coy, who had mopped up small marauding parties of enemy riflemen on the way up.

Lieut Oldings platoon and the leading troop of tanks were ordered to counter attack. The armour went in, saturating all the hedges and bushes in the area with concentrated fire. Soon, the rest of the column arrived, and the tanks turned their attention on the enemy occupied hump. The Germans answered with their 88s, in addition to the mortar fire, and life became somewhat more precarious on the ridge. Something had to be done to break the deadly stalemate. I devised a plan and discussed it with Lieut Col Osborne-Smith, CO of the Worcester's, who was with me.

Subject to confirmation by the Brigade Commander, 5DCLI would clear the left edge of the ridge, including the troublesome hump, while the Worcester's would capture Berjou. While our conference was taking place, the enemy SP guns and mortars fell strangely quiet, as if trying to guess our next move. During this eerie silence, every ear in the small and shallow trenches around us was centred on the discussion. The most welcome new arrival was Cpl Northcott, the mess corporal, who had braved the battle to get hot food to us. All at once on that ridge there was a picnic atmosphere, and one almost forgot that a few minutes earlier men were being killed under a rain of mortar bombs. A rather apprehensive Junior Staff officer sent forward by Essame – sweating from his climb, arrived.

As he related afterwards, I gave him a mug of tea and he realised that the situation was not as critical as he had thought. Soon after, Brigadier Essame approved my plan and confirmed that increased fire power would be available to support the Worcester's attack. A Coy, with Lieut B.M. Williams and J. Olding commanding it's platoons, took the ridge, supported by tanks, and a large number of the enemy were killed and captured in the process. In a farm on the plateau lay the bodies of five of our men. Around them were 19 dead Germans. Covered by the great artillery barrage, the Worcester's swept forward, taking Berjour and a considerable number of prisoners. One of the sights that remains with me was that of RSM Heard his face beaming with pleasure as he brought in 30 of the enemy at the double. As he passed, he threw me a parade ground salute. I knew him well as he was RSM of the Worcester's. Heard was a soldier of the old school, and fear was something with which he was not acquainted. He simply would not take cover, however intense the enemy shelling.

It was with great sorrow that we heard a few minutes later

he had been killed by an 88 shell. I was sure that he was over 50 years of age. Later in the afternoon, the whole battalion sidestepped to the left to exploit the success west of the Nerjou-Le-Hamel road. A small village to the south of the road was found to be unoccupied but mined. As it was in a hollow, we covered it from high ground until the position could be consolidated. Early next morning, our scout patrol of Sgt Dean and two men brought back two prisoners of 986 Grenadier Regt. During the night, Dean and his men had come across a party of 30 Germans sleeping near the road.

They had gently kicked the two into wakefulness and whisked them away. Dean later went back with reinforcements to collect the rest of the party; but the enemy had disappeared, no doubt mystified at the disappearance of their two comrades.

Later that day, we made contact with the Somerset's, who had captured Le Hamel. Our Pioneer Platoon, under Lieut Birchenall was kept busy for most of the remainder of the day clearing mines from the road. The crossing of the River Noireau and the capture of Berjou Ridge by the Brigade had been a fine feat of arms. Top commanders later being driven over the ridge expressed astonishment at its formidable nature as a defensive position.

The battalions losses in its capture were 16 killed, 17 wounded and two missing. The Sherwood Rangers had one tank destroyed, and one damaged. Two crew members had been killed by enemy snipers while gallantly going to rescue wounded comrades. The co-operation of the tanks, commanded by Captain Jack Homan, himself a Cornishman, had been excellent, and the happiest relations developed between the infantry and the Sherwood Rangers. This was to be the last action fought by 214 Brigade in Normandy. In an astonishingly short time, this place which had been battled over so ferociously and where so many men had died became a peaceful 'Back' area except for the tremendous volume of traffic, infantry and armour, pouring southwards in pursuit of the Germans.

The Canadians had taken Falaise on August 16 and the Americans Argentan. The jaws of the trap were closing on the doomed Germans but too slowly in the face of stiff resistance and by the 20th some of the toughest and most determined had got clear of the trap. Meanwhile, the British Second Army and the American 1st Army, strongly supported by the Tactical Air Forces, overran and eliminated the bulk of the fleeing enemy forces. Thus ended the battle of Normandy. For the British and Canadians the pivot on which the great battle had turned, it had been a hard and testing time, probably covering the most intense fighting in the west of the whole war. The Americans on the right of the British Army had also fought stoutly and their casualties were even greater than ours. Now under General Patton they were brilliantly exploiting the great success of the Allied Victory. Commented by General Sir Brian Horrocks:

"Nevertheless despite the slaughter in the Falaise Pocket claimed everywhere and rightly, as an outstanding victory one third of the German Army managed to withdraw many of them without equipment, had managed to escape before the encircling prongs had closed round them. This should not have happened: many reasons have been put forward for this, but to my mind no Germans would have escaped if Bradley had not halted Patton's northerly advance."

As an example of what an infantry battalion had to endure in such a campaign 5DCLI had fought almost continuously from June 26 until August 17.

Our losses bore grim witness to this a great proportion on Hill 112, 37 officers (120 per cent!) killed and wounded and 508 other rank casualties. The brunt being borne by the rifle companies. But Hitler, four years after his tanks had torn so devastatingly through France, had suffered a mortal blow. 43 of his divisions had been eliminated or severely mauled, and a number of others were bottled up in Brittany and the Channel Islands, to be captured at a later date. German losses were appalling: nearly half a million men the elite of the Nazi army . . . killed, wounded or taken prisoner. Some 1,500 enemy tanks had been destroyed and 3,500 guns were out of action or captured. It was General Montgomery was to tell the troops, on August 21 a "definite, complete and decisive victory". On a peaceful, sunny day, in stark contrast to the horrors of a short time earlier, we buried our dead behind the little farmhouse on the eastern edge of the ridge. Padre Gibbons conducted the simple, moving service, and the haunting notes of the last post sounded, carried over the fields ripe with corn for the harvest and followed by notes of hope in the inspiring Reveill and comrades of the fallen heaped flowers on the humble graves as buglers sounded *The Last Post*. Some corner of a foreign field. . .

CHAPTER FIVE

Across the Seine

The battle of Normandy was over. Our victory had indeed been "definite, decisive and complete". The evidence was there for all to see: wrecked German tanks, SP guns, trucks, half-trucks and wagons littered the roads; the French peasants moved unconcernedly among the stinking bodies of German troops and horses that lined the roads for miles.

Now all eyes turned to the Seine. It was to this French river that the Germans planned to withdraw in hope of preventing what was left of their Fifth and Seventh armies from again being surrounded. General Thomas received his orders from General Horrocks on the evening of 22 August: he was to cross the Seine three days hence to form a bridgehead of sufficient depth to allow the passage through of the remainder of the Corps and to protect its left flank between the rivers Eure and Seine.

Meanwhile the men of 5DCLI were resting and recovering from their recent ordeal. The weather was fine and hot, and we took the opportunity of bathing in the sun dappled cooling waters of the Noireau over which we had so bitterly fought.

General Thomas addressed the assembled troops of the brigade in a hollow square near battalion headquarters. He stressed the importance of the early capture of the V-bomb bases in the Pas de Calais which, since June, had been plaguing the people of southern England. But it was no summer holiday. Training was not forgotten and a short NCO's cadre was started. Then came the order that we were to move.

We celebrated with a party, and the noise of singing and jollification was heard far into the night. Sgt Grigg being the star entertainer. Next morning, thoroughly refreshed, the battalion moved forward to Gace, to protect the left flank of 129 Brigade, who were to move on to the Seine. We took up tactical positions near a pleasant French Country town. But the likelihood of hostile action was so remote we thought that the companies in turn held drill parades on the square under RSM Bishop.

I had the honour at this time of being invited to dine with Lieut General (later Sir Miles) Dempsey, Commander of the 2nd Army, who had set up his advanced tactical headquarters within the battalion area.

I had served on his staff at the beginning of the war, and was able to appreciate his general alertness and controlled nervous energy in the hour of exploitation of the great triumph of Falais.

Among the subjects we discussed that night was the amount of time a battalion should be given to stage an attack against an organised defensive position.

The General summed it up succinctly: "Two hours, only 50% success; four hours, 100% success."

Next day, the battalion was on the move again. At the start point, General Montgomery, from his open car, spoke to me, Bill Gorman, and some of the men. He looked remarkably fit, considering the strain he must have been through in the past few months. His fine eyes and sharp face were aglow with health. His ADC handed out boxes of cigarettes to the battalion. In the high noon of a summers day, we motored steadily through the lovely plains of France. Our destination was Vernon, on the Seine, where General Thomas was to force the crossing. Paris had been captured and US armoured patrols were pushing west and north. The shattered enemy remnants were struggling to cross the river.

It was vital for the Allies to breach the barrier of the Seine before the enemy could cross and reorganise in strength. A number of crossing places had been selected for the British and Canadian armies, and one on the extreme right was given to 43 Wessex Division.

The General was philosophical on receiving his orders to cross the river. He said: "This is the sort of operation the Staff College would lay down that a fortnight's planning would be necessary to ensure success. We have got to plan and get it right in a few hours!" He then retreated to his caravan, where he wrestled with the problem for eight hours!

It was in the cool of the evening when the leading elements of the battalion met Major Andy Martin, officer commanding Harbour Party at Pacy Sur Eure. The Harbour Party guides led the battalion quickly and efficiently into its Assembly area, a large wood some two miles north west of Pacy.

We were six miles from the river, but already we could hear the noisy grumble and thud of distant battle. The country looked lovely in the fading light of that glorious summer's day; it was difficult to imagine that soon we would be engaging the enemy in bloody conflict again, we felt as if we were on an exercise in Hampshire.

After supper, Brigadier Essame briefed us on the coming day's operations in a farmhouse which bore the scars of a recent skirmish between an American armoured patrol and a party of Germans. Already, he said, the Wiltshire's and 4th Somerset's of 129 Bde were forcing their way across the river, within two hours of arriving at Vernon after a mechanised march of some 120 miles.

The situation was till obscure, and it was not then known if we had secured a firm bridgehead. Briefly, the plan for the coming day was for the two remaining brigades of the division to pass through 129 Bde; 130 Bde on the right would exploit the right of the main road running north west of the Vernon Forest, and 214 Bde the left. We of the 5DCLI would be the leading battalion, and would move to Panaluise.

Dawn broke fine and clear after a peaceful night spent in the woods. The news came that three of the division's battalions had successfully crossed the river during the night. The 1st Worcester's, under the command of 129 Bde, had got across over the smashed bridge and were now mopping up in Vernonnet pockets of Germans who were still holding out on the cliffs above the village. The fire from these enemy positions were making the construction of a folding bridge by the Royal Engineers a difficult and costly operation. Shortly after breakfast I went forward to reconnoitre and found a good viewpoint on the high ground on the western edge of Vernon. Looking from the windows of a luxurious French villa, past the beautiful and clean town over the broad river, it was difficult to realise that men were killing and maiming each other on the far side. We could hear the boom and crack of our 25 pounders, and smoke could be seen billowing into the blue morning sky above Vernonnet.

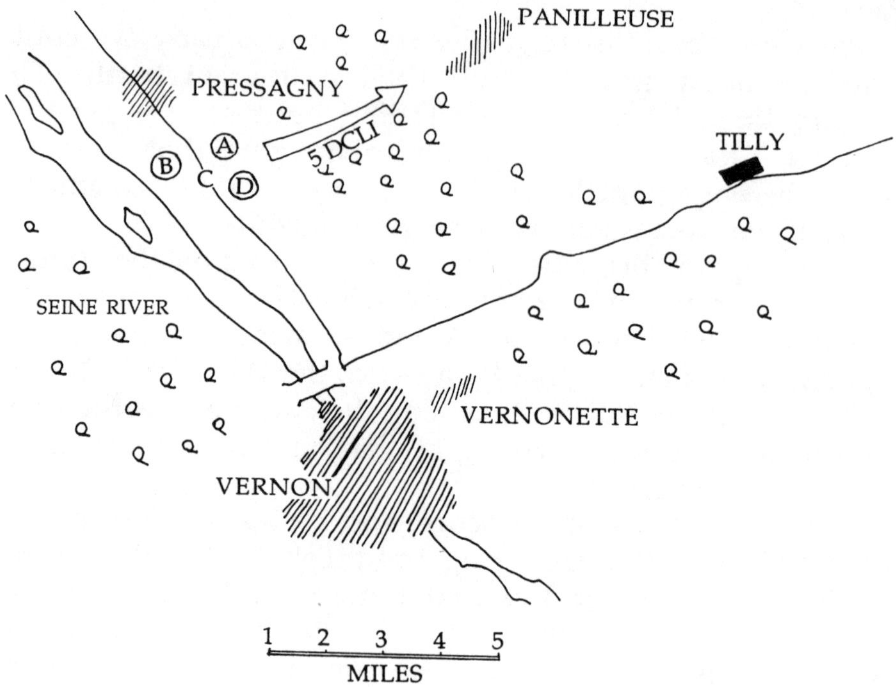

Our Scout Platoon radioed back that they were across the river and in touch with 4 Somerset's. I had sent them off earlier as a battle patrol under Captain Spencer with the object of locating the enemy. If there was no opposition, they were to move to the edge of the forest south of Panalieuse and remain there in an observation role until the battalion arrived.

Captain Anslow, with his Carrier Platoon, was instructed as part of the divisional plan to make a diversionary attack 10 miles to the northwest in the general direction of Les Andelys, to draw the enemy's reserves.

His small force consisted of a 25 pounder, a detachment of mortars, and a section of carriers. At noon, I and David

Willocks met the brigadier at 129 Bde HQ. He told us that the Somerset's were having difficulty in clearing the Germans from the cliffs above Vernonnet, and that the DCLI were to prepare to cross the Seine in DUKWS to lend support.

At 13.15 hours, we received orders to move into Vernon, an hour later, the battalion was assembled in the town, the men and vehicles hidden from the low flying enemy reconnaissance fighters by the tall thick trees that lined the road and which also supplied welcome shade from the hot sun. Two hours later, Scout Platoon reported that they had reached the centre of the Forest without encountering any opposition and were moving on to their final bound at the edge of the woods.

I took this important news to the divisional and brigade commanders, whom we met on the main road just outside the town. At about the same time, the Somerset's reported that they had completed their mopping up of nests of enemy machine gunners and snipers on the cliffs.

The role of the battalion was then altered: we were to cross the river, the marching troops moving by the broken bridge and the vehicles following by the 'class 9' bridge, now being completed by the industrious sappers, who were no longer under enemy bombardment.

Our particular task was to hold the left flank of the bridgehead by occupying a position in the area of Pressaguy L'Orgeilleux, while our original role would be taken over by the 7 Somerset's.

Our advance was turned into something of a festive occasion by the villagers of Vernonnet, who pressed wine and cider on the heavily laden infantrymen.

But despite these distractions, the column moved steadily forward. The celebrations had been a warning to us . . . on reaching the forest, south east of Pressaguy L'Orgeilleux I decided not to enter the village for fear that the welcome would be too great a temptation and cause men to relax their vigilance. Accordingly, B Coy, under Major Hingston, took up a position to the left of the high ground on the outskirts of the village: Major Parker's A Coy moved in on the right, in front of the forest edge, while D Coy was given the task of blocking the cross-tracks some 500 yards south east of Parker. Because of the Normandy casualties, C Coy had ceased to exist until we could get more reinforcements. Anti-tank guns were sited to cover the main approaches, and battalion headquarters was set up in the Chateau on the main road, which had been turned into a home for orphan boys. It was run by a bearded monk, who greeted us with an effusive show of hospitality. Later, he was to be arrested as a collaborator, and we learned that he had been unfrocked by the church for past misdeeds. All was quiet and peaceful as the battalion settled in, guarded by its patrols and sentry groups. Our bliss was to be short lived.

In the middle of the night, battalion HQ was startled by the news that part of B Coy had been overrun and that an enemy force was in the village. Captain Spencer was sent to investigate with a small escort and, if necessary, to take over command of B Coy.

It was not until 0300 hours that the situation was clarified. A patrol from B Coy, returning through the village, were met on the road by Major Hingston. He noticed shadowy figures moving behind them and called on them to identify themselves. Confusion broke out in all directions. The patrol had unknowingly picked up an enemy 'tail', and here they were, inside B Coy lines! A bren gun covering the road jammed at the crucial moment and it became a deadly game of hide and seek in the general melee to identify friend from foe in the darkness.

Then all was quiet until just before dawn. Under cover of darkness, the Germans had moved up through a field of corn to where a section of B Coy were holding a road junction leading to the high ground. Now, in superior numbers, swept out of the early morning mist and quickly overrun the few defenders. The survivors fell back to the A Coy positions just in front of the forest's edge. Firing rifles and light automatics and throwing grenades, the enemy stormed through the gap. Some continued down the road while a strong party outflanked A Coy platoons and began to assemble noisily in a hollow about 30 yards from the main body of Major Parker's men. But the mist and semi-darkness, which had been the Germans ally, now turned against them. In their haste, they had failed to notice the hidden defenders in their slit trenches, a mere 10 yards away.

At that range, they were sitting targets. CSM Philp took out several of them with one burst of his Bren; he then accounted for a machine gun team that had failed to notice him a few feet away when it had hurriedly positioned itself to concentrate its fire in the direction of battalion headquarters.

Harry Parker, crouched with his men under the very noses of the German advance party, gave the whispered word of command to cease firing, and then called me on the phone to explain his desperate position. I discussed a plan quietly over the telephone with Harry to bring down the fire of our supporting artillery on his position, he bravely agreed and I got through to the artillery, this bold stroke succeeded. The first salvo sent the enemy scurrying into the woods, helped on their way by two magazines of the redoubtable C.S.M. Philps' bren gun. The common sense reasoning behind Major Parker's agreement was borne-out by the fact that we suffered only three casualties from the artillery fire. The slit trenches had afforded excellent protection. But two prisoners taken by the Germans had been murdered in cold blood. The drama was not over. It was now D Coys turn, as the enemy estimated at two companies, moved into the cross-tracks area some 500 yards away.

A small detachment held them up for a short time in a bloody little action, but after inflicting losses on the enemy, they were overrun and every man killed. For a while, there was confusion among the men of D Coy, and stragglers fell back to Battalion HQ. But the enemy column, identified from a dead German officer as 148 Grenadier Regt, had disappeared mysteriously into the wood. Our spirits rose somewhat with the arrival of several armoured cars from the Divisional Recce Regt. They were a welcome reinforcement as the battalion area was a difficult position to hold, owing to its wooded nature and the fact that we had only three rifle companies. Later in the morning, we were further strengthened by a few tanks and advanced without further incident to occupy the village of Pressinguy, in a defensive role. But any hopes of a respite were quickly dashed. Next day, we were relieved by tired Worcestershire's, who with the Somerset's had been involved in heavy fighting. It was with regret that we felt the comfortable little village, our last act being to provide a firing party at the burial of a Frenchman who had been killed by the Germans. We plunged into the forest with orders to capture Panillieuse, some 4 miles away which was necessary to complete the bridgehead. The trees and undergrowth were thick, and we were forced to advance in a long 'snake'. I felt that we were in danger of being ambushed like General Braddocks Red Coats were in the American War of Independence.

It was with relief that I, with Major Fry, OC of D Coy, which was leading, reached the north east edge of the forest. Ahead of us, we saw Germans and French civilians moving around a large farm.

There was no way round it. My problem was whether to call in artillery covering fire, inflicting possible casualties on the French, or to advance without it, putting my own men in danger.

The latter was out of the question: so a warning salvo would be put down short of the target to allow the locals to get under cover. After the softening-up barrage, I sent in D Coy, supported by tanks of the Sherwood Rangers. The Germans quickly deserted their positions round the farm and fled towards the village. But not before killing two of our men with a small mortar bomb fired from a clump of trees. Ironically, also we had one man wounded . . . by one of our own shells falling short and hitting the tops of the trees at the edge of the wood. After quick reconnaissance from the farm, it was decided to use B Coy to spearhead the attack on Panillieuse. Their leading Platoon, under cover of artillery and mortar fire, occupied a small orchard to the south east of the village, and then provided covering fire while the rest of the company swept through with great dash into the village. Such was their determination, that they went through our own shell fire to get at the enemy. Lieut

Bishop and four privates were slightly wounded by our own guns.

But the enemy, lying low in their slit-trenches, were caught unawares by the onslaught, and four of them were killed and several others taken prisoner. A number of others were chased in the fading light through the village streets. A house to house search for any remaining German troops was considerably hampered by French residents, who welcomed our men with open arms, thrusting flowers upon them, kissing the somewhat embarrassed soldiers, and plying them with wine.

One gloriously intoxicated Frenchman, who kept roaring out 'Le Marseilleise' insisted on throwing his arms around the necks of our officers and had to be put under restraint!

By the light of a burning building, our position was consolidated. The laconic message 'Panillieuse captured' was the signal for the great armoured drive by the armoured division of the British Army under Horrocks to start over the Somme battlefields of the past and on to the liberation of Brussels, and that great strategic prize, the deep water port of Antwerp. To sustain this advance, most of the transport of 43 Division was taken away and we were left in peace on the green and wooded banks of the Seine.

With good news coming in from all fronts, optimism was in the air. Little did we realise then that much tough fighting was still to come. But we made the best of things. Billetted in the big farms and in the village itself, all ranks soon became on friendly terms with the inhabitants. Dances were arranged and ENSA nights were a great attraction. Stars like Flanagan and Allen, Florence Desmond, Kay Kavendish and Richard (Mr Pastry) Hearne helped bring light relief into the lives of the fighting men.

Somewhat ahead of official sanction, a party of officers visited Paris . . . probably the first British liberating troops into the French capital. Later, parties of all ranks were organised to visit this city once renowned for its gaiety. The story was told in the Division of one of our Padres, who walking down the Champilesy in the Capital, when he was spotted by our General, who was visiting Paris to make official arrangements for parties to visit it. The General sent his staff officer across the road who said, "Padre, what are you doing here?" Back came the quick answer, "Buying communion wine, sir".

Life blood began to flow back into the battalion with the arrival of fresh drafts or reinforcements, and soon it was strong enough to reorganise itself into four rifle companies again. I am strongly of the opinion that on mobilization a battalion should have four rifle companies, instead of the present three.

C Coy was resurrected under the capable and steady hands of Major Kitch (Kitchen), by then recovered from his Normandy wounds. Most of the newcomers were youngsters, aged about 20. Now back at strength, we could afford to turn our attention to matters of a lighter nature while awaiting our next assignment. Our 'big game' hunter, Major Hingston, organised a boar hunt in the forest of Vernon. However, the nearest the party came to their quarry was a sleeping wild pig that one of the hunters stumbled over. The startled animal broke through the hunters' ranks and got clean away. Those golden, happy days of early autumn were passing all too quickly. And soon there was talk of the Division moving into the Low Countries.

CHAPTER SIX

Breakthrough to Driel near Arnhem

Montgomery's great victory in Normandy had cost the German Army half a million men which included over 200,000 prisoners and a mass of equipment a greater toll than they had suffered at Stalingrad. Now, Monty was strongly advocating that a force of some 40 British US and Canadian divisions under his command should at once force a crossing of the Rhine and advance across the German northern plain to Berlin.

Had the British commander had his way, and the envisaged supply problems overcome, the tough winter fighting that was to come could perhaps have been avoided, and the hundreds of thousands of casualties avoided. The war could have been over by Christmas, 1944.

But for two blissful weeks, as the glorious sunny days of late summer moved drowsily towards the autumn, it seemed to us of 5DCLI that hostilities were at an end. The atmosphere was one of peacetime soldiering in our billets on the edge of the Vernon forest. What some of our soldiers, in fact, called a cushy number.

The killing and suffering of the past weeks seemed remote during those golden, happy autumn days, and the news of the successful sweep of Allied armour into Belgium and Holland was so good that we began to believe the battalion would not be called upon again to play its part in the grim game of war. Then, on the morning of September 14, shrouded in the first cold mists of autumn, it all changed. We were on the move again. This time, to Holland.

The route followed was Breteuil, Beauvais, Albert, skirting Brussels, from thence off to Mons and leading us past the battlefields over which our fathers and elder brothers had contested with the same Teutonic foe.

It was a perfect September day as we quickly passed through open rolling country of the Somme. After skirting Brussels, we came upon the sea-borne trail of the 1st

Airborne Division, which gave us a hint of what lay ahead. The Belgians gave us a great welcome. At Briane Le Conte, our resting place for the night, we were received with hospitality, the good burghers housing our men for the night. Battalion Headquarters was located in a Monastery School. The monks told us stories of the SS troops, who had retreated through the town on bicycles and a miscellaneous collection of transport. Next day we journeyed on to Diest. Along the route we noticed a considerable amount of wrecked German transport, victims of our air superiority. On arriving at Diest, we moved to our concentration area just northeast of the town. We were not allowed to spread ourselves and it was evident from the number of troops in the concentration area that serious business was afoot.

The next day I attended a conference in the theatre of Diest, where Generals Dempsey and Horrocks lucidly gave out the bold plan for 'Operation Market Garden' to the assembled Generals, Brigadiers and Commanding Officers of 30 Corps. During the course of the afternoon the outline plan was explained to all officers of the Battalion. The next day, the 17th, after Brig. (now Maj-Gen) Essame had given out brigade orders, I then, with the aid of a huge diagram, outlined the bold and dramatic plan to the assembled Battalion. The object was to secure a bridgehead over the Rhine. This entailed the crossing of three great rivers, the Maas, the Waal and the Neder Rijn at Arnhem. The airborne troops of three magnificent Divisions:- 101 US Airborne Division Major General Mazwell Taylor 82 US Airborne Division Major General Gavin, 1st British Airborne Division Major General Urquhart, were to pave the way by forming a 'flying carpet' and seizing the great bridges at Grave, Nijmegen and Arnhem. Montgomery's first thought on the plan was to use the 1st British Airborne Division to secure the first part of the 60 mile route to Arnhem and the two American Airborne Divisions to secure the great Bridge at Nijmegen and Arnhem. At a preplanning meeting with General Oman Bradley the American commander of the US 1st Army. Bradley pointed out the great risks to the American Division that was to be dropped near Arnhem.

Therefore Montgomery decided to use the British 1st Airborne Division in this role – though it was not as tidy or as logical as his original plan.

The 2nd Army, with 30 corps as its steel spearhead, was then to connect up with the airborne troops with the utmost speed.

The guards Armoured Division was to lead 30 Corps and the 43 Division was to pass through after the capture of Arnhem and reach the Apeldoorn area, blocking the escape routes of the German armies in Holland. As the main points of the plan began to sink into the minds of the men, who sat on the grass at my feet, there was a roar of amazement and wonder: one could feel the different reactions.

Some were delighted by its very boldness, and flushed with excitement, others were slightly perturbed and some very cynical, but in general the mass felt that the Battalion could give a good account of itself in the adventures that lay ahead of us. Active preparations began at once. Strict MT discipline was stressed. The maximum use of the single road by packing vehicles nose to tail, and by keeping a clear lane for returning traffic was to be of vital importance.

'Dukws' arrived during the evening of this day to act as transport carriers for the Battalion.

Next morning the Battalion moved forward to the transit area in the woods near Hechtel. On arrival, the time was spent in studying our task by the aid of a big sand-model.

Apeldoorn, our objective, was a very wooded area, and the platoons practised wood-fighting. Special emphasis was laid on defence and counter-attack. Tanks were to work with the reserve platoons of forward companies, and were to act bodly in defence staying at night with the forward troops and not withdrawing to a rear rally as laid down in the textbook.

News was received that the operation was going as planned. The sight of the great armadas in the sky had an exhilarating effect on us all. The night of September 19 was spent peacefully in the transit area, except for a hostile night bombing attack on the Brigade area.

We were at short notice to move and during the course of the next afternoon we received our marching orders to move to Nijmegen, where the Guards and U.S. Para troops were fiercely engaged. During the night the Battalion threaded its way up the narrow 1,000 yard corridor held by American Airborne troops and British armoured regiments. A considerable number of farms on the flanks of the road were ablaze. The night was dark and gloomy as we found our way through the silent streets of Eindhoven, which was captured by the Guards Armoured Division and American Para Troops of General Gavin's 82 Airborne Division who with the 101 Airborne Division under General Maxwell Taylor played a splendid part in the whole battle. Morning broke clear and sparkling and found the column approaching Grave. There were many halts owing to the traffic. The Dutch gave us a great welcome, and brought us pails of fresh milk to drink. There was no news about how the 1st British Airborne Division was fairing.

I could not help thinking of the battle of KUT 1915 in Mespotania against the Turks. I remembered as a boy of 10 years how a British Indian Division under General Townsend had been besieged for a long time and how determined efforts to relieve them had all failed. No doubt it was the association in my mind with the great rivers of the Tigris and Euphratic Rivers in Mespotania now Iraq and the great rivers of North West Europe where we were now operating.

As we moved up the road we realised what a magnificent job General Maxwell Taylors, 101 Airborne Division had done, securing five of the six bridges over rivers and canals, the sixth bridge the enemy were able to blow in their faces. The American Engineers, with great energy and initiative, using timber from a Dutch Saw Mill, had quickly rebuilt it, so that the tanks of the Guards Armoured Division could use it. Later I was proud to serve under this fine commander.

General Gavins 82nd Airborne Division were of equal high quality. Owing to the fog on UK airfields their three Glider Infantry battalions were delayed, nevertheless the under strength 82nd fought off German attacks from the dark forest of the Reichwald, and with the Grenadier Guards played a big part in the capture of the Nijmegen Bridge. To do this a battalion of the 504 Regiment had to carry out an assault, crossing the fast flowing Waal River in daylight, using unfamiliar small British paddle assault boats. They were supported by the fire of the tanks of the Irish Guards. Against heavy enemy fire only half the boats carrying the first wave got across, but in spite of this they secured a foothold and gradually secured a bridgehead which enabled them to attack and capture the great Nijmegen Bridge and its guards. A number of senior British officers were witness to this very brave and brilliant episode. To quote Chester Wilmot: "Struggle for Europe". When General Dempsey the commander of the British 2nd Army met Gavin after this expolit he said: "I am proud to meet the commander of the greatest Division in the World today".

Whilst this was going on we reached Aluerna six miles from Nijmegen. I went ahead to carry out a recce from the Bridge with the Brigadier and the C.Os of the Brigade. They left me on the Bridge and it was here that I met General Horrocks, as usual well forward seeing things for himself. He told me that the enemy were beginning to recover their balance and was stubbornly holding a line north of the bridge and preventing the Guards breaking through to reach the hard pressed British Airborne Division at Arnhem.

General Model had made a good appreciation, to block the approach of the Guards as his first priority. The terrain between Nijmegen and Arnhem was a reclaimed and drained bog, limiting the use of tanks-thus favouring the German defensive lay out. Horrocks said, "What would you do George?" I said, "Do a left hook and use the Dukws to cross behind the enemy holding Oosterhoot," I did not believe that they had much depth behind that village. This proved to be so.

At first we thought that we would be ordered to cross over the river that afternoon, with a view to breaking through the enemy positions in a night attack. This was not to be, because the 7th Somerset Light Infantry in the lead were delayed having been misdirected by Dutch Guides in the town, and we were ordered to concentrate for the night on the north east side of Nijmegen. The 7th Somersets were ordered to attack Oosterhoot at 07.00 hrs next morning. It being the Brigadiers intention to reach Neder Rijn on this day. The night was spent restfully in the houses of the Dutch inhabitants, who received us with every kindness. The next day, September 22, broke fine and clear. The Battalion waited patiently all the morning in the streets of Nijmegen for the orders to advance. Meanwhile, the 7th Somerset Light Infantry had crossed the bridge and were engaged with the enemy near Oosterhoot. One of the difficulties that we had to face up to at this period of the operations was the limited amount of artillery ammunition available, and for this reason the 7th Somerset Light Infantry had to spend a great deal of time in finding out exactly where enemy strongpost were located before the precious artillery ammunition could be used.

The enemy resisted tenaciously the efforts of the advance guard Company, and it became obvious to the battalion commander of the 7th Somerset's Light Infantry, Lt Col Borrowdale, that a battalion attack with full scale artillery support would be necessary. The hour for this attack by the 7th Somerset's was fixed for 1600 hours. By that time Brigadier Essame had found enough artillery shells to do the job.

In the early afternoon the 5th Duke of Cornwall's Light Infantry moved over the railway bridge into an assembly area behind the big embankment near the 7th Somerset's. Meanwhile, I had been up to Lt-Col Borrowdale and made arrangements to pass through and exploit the success of the 7th Somerset's. To make co-operation fully effective the command posts of the two battalions were established within 50 yards of each other. At about this time a Staff Officer of 30 Corps came forward and told me that news had been received that the 1st British Airborne Division were in a desperate position, and that we must link up with them that night. Two 'Dukws' carrying ammunition and medical supplies were given to the battalion to be delivered to the airborne troops.

Final orders for the move through the 7th Somerset's were given in a ditch just below the embankment to the assembled company. The great risk of the operation was obvious to us all. However, it was made clear that nothing was going to be allowed to stop the 5th Duke of Cornwall's and the Squadron of 4/7th Dragoon Guards. Briefly, the plan was for B Company, under Major Hingston, acting as advance guard, to move through the Somerset's and under the cover of a short artillery barrage and smoke, to secure the area of the orchards to the west of the village: then D Company, with tank support, was to secure the area of the hamlet of Slijk Ewijk, and there to form a protective screen to cover the mounting of the remainder of the battalion on the tanks, carriers, anti tank guns, and 'Dukws' in readiness for a swift advance to the Rhine at Driel, where a Polish para Brigade was reported to be. The carrier platoon was to be used to piquet the side of the road with the object of giving the column some flank protection.

Under the cover of a heavy artillery barrage, the 7th Somerset's swept over the embankment to the attack. Soon news reached us of their success, and the command was given – advance. Prisoners, many of them wounded, and a pitiful sight, were being brought in by the Somerset's, as B Company felt its way forward, through the half shattered village. Rumours of enemy tanks caused them to move off the main road, and go through a tangle of gardens and orchards, which caused a slight delay and alteration in the artillery plan. Soon they were moving through the open country, clear of the village, on to their objectives – the orchards, protected by a hail of high explosives ripping up likely enemy positions. No sign of the enemy. Over the wireless I gave the order, "Push on, change of plan, seize D Company's objective," thus, time was to be saved.

Then through the village came the head of the main body of the Battalion, and we began to form up on the road on the north east of Oosterhoot. Before us lay a fleeting chance. Could we make it before the enemy recovered his balance. Disturbing news was received that two enemy tanks could be seen about 1,000 yards to the north. They had been located by Major John Fry and confirmed by the IO, Capt David Wilcox and myself. I told them not to pass on this information though I realised that there were probably more enemy tanks in the vicinity, as time was vital and no one should hesitate but I told Major Richards the squadron commander. After the battle we learnt that there were 20 enemy tanks and two infantry battalions near Elst. It was decided to ignore them.

ARNHEM 22nd SEPTEMBER 1944

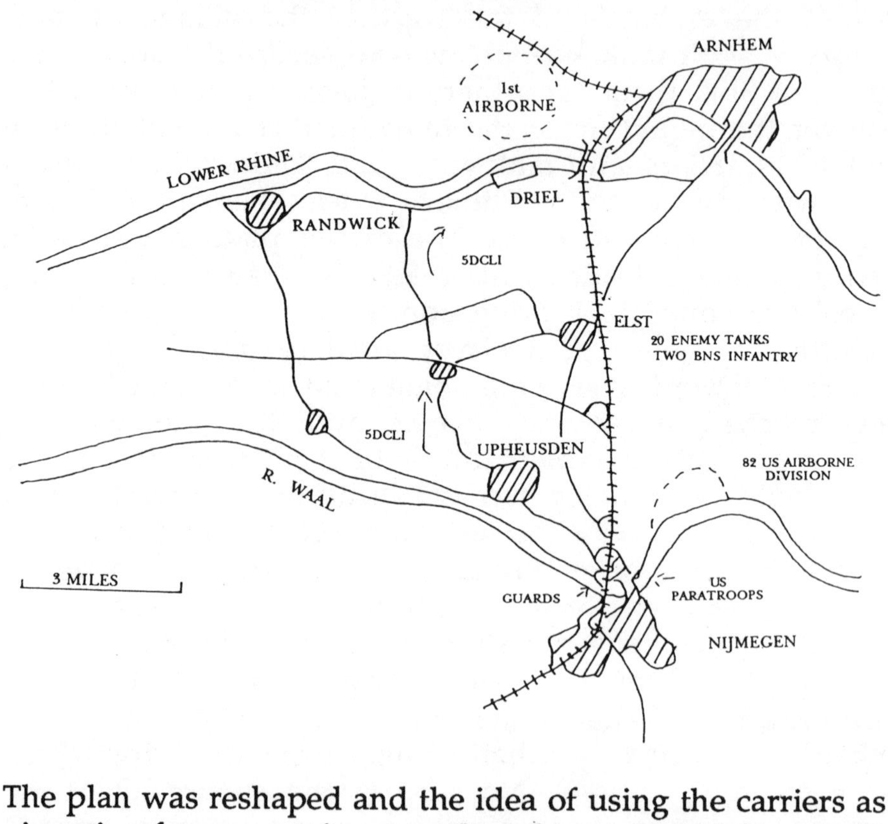

The plan was reshaped and the idea of using the carriers as a piqueting force was given up. Speed was essential more than ever, or the enemy would move his reserves to close the gap; also night was fast approaching and in the dark we would not be able to move more than a mile or so. The vital minutes were flying; we galvanised the slow-plodding platoons as they came forward from the village. Soon the men of the front part of the column were all mounted on tank, carrier or gun. The Battalion formed up as follows:

ARMOURED COLUMN

All personnel carried on carriers, anti-tank guns, etc.

Squadron 4/7th Dragoon Guards (Major Richards) with D Company (Major Fry) mounted on the tanks.

Command Group, 5th Duke of Cornwall's Light Infantry (CO and IO).

Carrier Platoon with Scout Platoon.

MMG Platoon, 8th Middlesex.

One Platoon, A Company, Duke of Cornwall's Light Infantry.

Two 'Dukws' (ammunition and medical stores).

One Platoon C Company, Duke of Cornwall's Light Infantry.

RA Carrier and Mortar Platoon A Company, Duke of Cornwall's Light Infantry, less one platoon (Major Parker's, section of 6-pdr anti-tank guns.

SOFT VEHICLE COLUMN
Personnel mainly on foot under the command of Major St George Martin

C Company, Duke of Cornwall's Light Infantry, less one platoon (Major Kitchen), section 6-pdr anti-tank guns and 333 Battery anti tank guns, 17 pdrs (Capt Bellamy).

B Company, Duke of Cornwall's Light Infantry (Major Hingston). Note: to follow on once tail column had passed Slijk Ewijk.

Off we moved, tracks clanking, motors roaring dashing-headlong, ignoring the danger of ambush and mines, we were soon in the streets of Valburg.

The Dutch inhabitants, somewhat astonished at this eruption of armour and men, went wild with joy, shouting and cheering till their lungs almost burst as we quickly moved on. The light was fading rapidly as the head of the column reached Driel tracks of the leading tank being blown up on a mine at the entrance leading to the village. The journey of about 10 miles had been completed in under 30 minutes. We felt that even General Patton would not grumble at this!

The sound of battle could not be heard behind the armoured column, and very shortly afterwards a DR came up to the Command Carrier and reported to me that enemy tanks were attacking the soft vehicle column. He had been standing at the cross roads between Valburg and Elst to direct traffic and seeing some tanks approach, he had signalled them on. A few seconds later, to his horror, he saw the dark German crosses on the tanks. Fortunately his motor cycle was just around the corner, facing the right direction and running to it, he moved up to Driel with all speed to report.

It was realised that in the darkness the troops of the soft vehicle column would have a very good chance of holding off the tank attack. The armoured column immediately took up positions of all round defence. I then turned my attention to the problems of linking up with the airborne troops and delivering the two 'Duwk' loads of supplies. By the light of a burning building contact was made with a troop of the Household Cavalry, who had daringly slipped through in the early morning mist; the Germans had neglected to barricade the road. Shortly afterwards Lt-Col McKenzie, the GI of the first Airborne Divisions, arrived, having swum the river. He outlined the situation of the first Airborne. They were hemmed in into a narrow perimeter, just to the west of Oosterbeck. Their losses had been heavy, so much so that they had hardly sufficient men to man the perimeter and were in urgent need of reinforcements. They were all very short of sleep, supplies and ammunition, though in the case of the latter, it was not quite so urgent as had been reported. The enemy was in great force, and were especially strong in armour (tanks and SP guns).

When asked about the road-bridge at Arnhem he said the position had been in our hands, but nothing had been heard for the last 24 hours from Frost's Battalion, and it looked as if they had been overwhelmed. My first reaction was to move the Battalion and to attack the roadbridge at Arnhem. This, however, after a further discussion with the GI Mackenzie was reluctantly abandoned because it was felt that it was extremely unlikely that we still held the bridge and that the enemy would be by now holding it in strength. It was necessary to try and reinforce firstly, the perimeter with men and secondly with supplies and thirdly it was also necessary to prevent the enemy getting round on the south side of the perimeter and finally sealing it off. Later we heard that the gallant holders of the bridge, having exhausted their ammunition with the cellars full of wounded and the houses about the bridge a seething mass of flame, had surrendered 24 hours before our arrival at Driel.

Frost, the Commander of the 2nd Para Battalion in this epic of heroic resistance, has since told me how well the German SS Troops treated his wounded men, giving them brandy and chocolate. Touch was then obtained with the Polish HQ in the middle of the village. Although called a brigade the Polish force was only equivalent to about a battalion in strength.

A conference was now held between the brigade commander of the Polish Brigade, Gen Sosobowski, and Eddie Myers CRE 6f 1st British Airborne Division and myself. It was reported at this time that the Polish Brigade were ferrying by rafts and a small boat, reinforcements of Poles across the river, and it was decided that these reinforcements should have priority and that nothing be done with the 'Dukws' that might give away the passage of these reinforcements over the river. The approximate time for the 'Dukws' to go over was fixed for 0200 hours. Air photos of the river were studied with great care and the two RASC 'Dukw' drivers with the IO did a recce of the obstacles and the river bank. They were of the opinion that it was just possible, the obstacles being the narrow roads which had ditches on both sides, the high bund and a narrow dike.

The Pioneer Platoon and the 'Dukws' were put under the command of the GI who had with him the CRE of the 1st British Airborne for the operation of trying to surmount the obstacles and getting the 'Dukws' over. A series of stops were put out by the scout platoon to prevent the enemy patrols interfering with the operation.

Just before the head of the column had made contact with the Poles, exciting events had happened to the rear part of A Company, and to the soft vehicle column. Major Parker, bringing up the rear of his company, in his jeep, followed by his two company carriers and a 15-cwt truck, reached the DeHook cross-roads when suddenly a tank column came round the corner from Elst.

Major Parker had passed the first tank before he realised that they were Germans. He then drove with all speed towards Driel, to report and join up with the rest of his company. Behind the jeep came the first carrier, containing C.S.M. Philp, Pte Tucker, the driver, and some others.

ACCOUNT BY C.S.M. PHILP, DCM

"Major Parker was leading A Company's group of vehicles in his jeep, but was travelling at too great a speed for my carrier and by the time we were half way to Driel, I was 600 yards behind, and the carrier following behind was another 200 yards away.

In the distance I saw Major Parker passing a tank, on the fork roads between Elst and Driel, but I carried on as I failed to realise that they were Germans. When I was within 100 yards, I saw that they were a column of tanks, and, what was more important, they were all marked with the black cross. We could not stop, but charged on, hoping to get through. The first two tanks pulled over to the right of the road and we skidded to a standstill with the front of the carrier touching the front of the tank. At the time I was sitting on the top of the carrier with a light machine gun on my lap. The tank commander leaned out of the turret and commenced to remove his goggles, so I immediately gave him a burst with my LMG and he slithered down inside the turret. At the same time the German crew opened fire with the two machine guns, but as one was too low and the other too high we did not suffer any casualties, and we all baled out to the right and left of the road. As I sent to jump from the carrier, I still clearly remember striking my head on the 88 millimetre gun of the tank. We were very lucky, as on each side of the road was a ditch containing mud and reeds, which afforded excellent cover. From this ditch I observed five Tiger Tanks on the road above us, and about a dozen enemy infantry on road about 100 yards away. Pte Rogers and myself, using the cover afforded by the ditch and the failing light, managed to contact the remainder of the column which was in the rear, approximately one mile behind. I then informed Major Kitchen of the occurrence and the enemy's position."

Meanwhile the rear carrier, containing Lt Olding of A Company had turned back and met Lt Bellamy with his anti tank guns. They immediately got the guns into position ready for action, and waited until Major Kitchen came up with C Company. The latter made a rapid appreciation and decided to detour. This was successfully carried out and Major Kitchen arrived in the vicinity of rear Battalion Headquarters at 2100 hours, meanwhile, Major Parker had reported the situation to me, the DR's report had made me aware of the situation and having discussed the matter with Harry Parker decided to ambush the Tiger Tanks. He borrowed a number of Piats and 75' type mines from the rest of the battalion and went to set up the ambush. On the way back he met Major Kitchen and got a further report of the situation. It was appreciated that by now the tanks would probably be in contact with B Company.

(Major Parker's story) AMBUSH OF THE TIGERS

We moved down the road and I dropped one Platoon half-way between the De Hoop cross roads and Driel as a firm base. The tanks could be heard milling about in the distance, towards where I thought B Company were. I considered that sooner or later they would come back down the road to Elst and that the best place to intercept them would be the De Hoop cross-roads. Accordingly, we set our trap. I gave orders for complete silence and nor rounds to be fired unless attacked by infantry because of the flash. Piats to be fired in a volley of three when given the order. No firing to take place until the leading tank had hit the mines. We now heard German Tiger tanks shooting up B Company and as this was happening a German motor combination came up the road from Elst, presumably to contact the tanks.

He blew up literally on our 75 mines. Next, we heard the tanks returning headed by a DR. He also blew up. The leading tank was firing Verey lights to light the way every 30 seconds. It was fairly obvious that they were 'windy'. There were five tanks. As the first tank reached the 75 mines, I gave orders for groups two and three to fire. There was a tremendous explosion and six Piat bombs hit the tank. This put him completely out of action. The next tank hit the mines and received the same treatment. The third tank tried to back out, but hit a string of mines which had been pulled in behind it and came to a halt on the initial explosion, and every time he tried to move another mine went off.

Eventually he too, was knocked out by Pte Brown, who went within a few yards of the tank with his Piat before he fired. The tank was out, but so was one of the eyes of the Piat firer. The last words of Brown as he was put on the jeep and lost consciousness were 'I don't care I knocked the so-and-so thing out'. It was his first action. He was proud of it. Brown was later awarded the Military Medal for this gallant action.

The two remaining tanks behind panicked and tried to back out in a hurry. They both ditched themselves in the deep ditch which ran along side the road. The crews escaping into the woods. The company was then reorganised, C.S.M. Philp first making sure that every tank was incapable of further action by dropping grenades down the turrets. This he did whilst exposed to heavy shell fire. For, attracted by the should of the explosion and burning tanks, our own artillery shelled the cross-roads and a shell splinter wounded the stout hearted C.S.M. in the face. He, however, resolutely carried on with his task.

The Company was then organised for a withdrawal, our task being completed, we moved back to the Battalion at Driel.

At 0200 hours the 'Dukw' party, under the command of the GI British Airborne Division, and guided by the Battalion Intelligence Officer started on their journey to the river bank. The narrow road was slippery with a recent down pour of rain, and the night extremely dark. In addition to these difficulties as they got nearer to the river, the 'Dukws' ran into heavy ground mist and in spite of the greatest care, the big awkward vehicles slipped off the road in the ditches just short of the river.

It was then suggested that the relief stores and some of the ammunition should be transferred to the raft that had been taking the Poles across. The idea was turned down as it was considered that as many reinforcements as possible be sent over before the early morning light would put a stop to the slow flow of men across the river.

Meanwhile B Company was still missing. It had spent the night in trying to find a way through the thin cordon of enemy posts which the enemy had promptly established behind the bulk of the Battalion. In the end its Company Commander had decided to take his weary mud-bespattered men back to Swijk-Wwijk, where he had met Major Martin, the second-in-command who had brought up additional supply 'Dukws'. They remained in defensive positions till next morning.

The Battalion during the early morning laid on a fire plan to assist the hard pressed airborne troops, and all that day the tanks, the MGs, Brens, and our 3-in mortars kept up an intermittent fire at the enemy, who was pressing into the flanks of the 1st Airborne. All the 3-in mortar ammunition was used for this purpose. If we could not carry it across we would throw it across. The medical stores and some of the lighter ammunition were to be ferried across by the Poles that night. The enemy replied to our fire with a considerable number of 88 shells and mortar bombs, including many airbursts, Lt-Col McKenzie, the GI of the Airborne, had early that morning gallantly tried to go back to Nijmegen to report to 30 Corps on the grave situation. At his first attempt, his armoured car was shot up by an enemy tank and he was lucky to escape with his life. We therefore gave him an escort of some tanks. These managed to give him enough covering fire to slip past the danger area and by the use of side roads, reach the Headquarters of 30 Corps.

A request was made to Brigade HQ for a supply of assault boats to be brought up with the relieving column so that the Battalion would if necessary, be able to cross the river. Meanwhile, the enemy stronghold at Elst had been partly cleared after heavy fighting by the Worcestershire's and Somerset's, under the command of Brig Essame; the way was now clear for the Division to come up and end our isolation. At about 1100 hours the leading elements of 130 Brigade Lt Col Code, 5th Dorset's, began to arrive and took up a position on the right of the Battalion facing the river. A few assault boats, brought up by 130 Brigade, were given to the Polish Brigade, who were to make a big effort to get reinforcements across the river that night. For this operation, the Battalion's fire resources were used to neutralise the enemy on the left flank of the bridgehead. The fire was the most effective and kept the enemy's fire down to a minimum. However mainly owing to the fact that the Polish troops were not very skilled in this type of operation, only about 200 of these stout-hearted fighters managed to get across.

General Horrocks

Early next morning the Corps Commander Lt-Gen Horrocks, arrived at Battalion HQ and heartily congratulated the Battalion on our break-through to link up with the airborne forces. It was at this time that he started to call the battalion the cream of the cream. The brigade in his opinion being the cream of our west country division. I went with him to a church tower in the village which we were using as an OP. He made a thorough reconnaissance of the ground, the position of the enemy and our own troops. Very shortly afterwards he was joined by the Division Commander, Maj-Gen Thomas (Lt-Gen Sir Ivor Thomas). A short discussion then took place on the best line of action of how to relieve or succour the hard pressed airborne troops. I was very relieved when we left the Church Tower one shell through it would most likely killed all of us.

There was great air activity this day. The attempts to drop supplies were tragic, but a wonderful spectacle of courage and devotion by the air crews, both American and British. Halifaxes and Dakotas, flying in compact groups against the angry black bursts of flak shells. Only a small percentage of the parachute containers fell in the target area. Our air losses were heavy. Because of poor radio communications corrections of the drops could not be made.

I anticipated that the Battalion might be called upon to cross the river that night. Therefore, a plan to do so was made out and the necessary reconnaissance were carried out during the course of the morning. This, however, was not to be, and the 4th Dorset's were selected for this hazardous task. After mid-day we took up fresh positions in the now rapidly forming Division salient from the positions in the vicinity of the railway line. This move brought to an end the Battalion's direct efforts to help the airborne troops.

Undoubtedly, but for the speed, determination and dash of the Battalion and of the squadron of 4/7th Dragoon Guards, the enemy troops from Elst, which were later estimated at two battalions of SS Infantry and 20 tanks, would have closed the gap and probably stopped, or at least greatly slowed up, the relief of the gallant remnants of the 1st Airborne Division, over 2,000 of whom were evacuated across the river on September 26.

The military lessons of the Operation might be said to be:

(1) Luck will often favour boldness. The very speed with which the Column moved ensured its safety and enabled it to reach the river. The head of the Column only avoided the enemy tanks by about six or seven minutes.

(2) Infantrymen imbued with a fighting spirit, if circumstances will allow them to get to close quarters, can defeat tanks. We had a lot of previous experience of dealing with tanks with the Piat. This undoubtedly added to our confidence. John Fry, Richards, Harry Parker, Philp and Brown all deserve great credit. And also my Intelligence officer David Willcocks. If we had delayed by only a few minutes. We would have been too late. And the enemy could have blocked the whole Brigade and none of the gallant 1st Airborne men could have been rescued.

At the present time (1990) our hand held anti-tank Infantry Weapons are almost useless against

Soviet tanks with their Explosive reactive ARMOUR. It is essential that we rearm our Infantry with a good anti-tank weapon, otherwise we will share the fate of the French Infanty in 1940 – who had no Infantry Weapons to deal with the Panzers.

CONCLUSIONS

There are a number of reasons for the Arnhem failure but probably the most important were:-

1. A general failure of radio communications – careful check to see that they would perform 100% does not seem to be made. This meant that our good reserves of air and landpower were not used or used too late.

2. A bolder plan to drop a battalion in the initial assault at Arnhem that is drop a battalion on or near the Arnhem Bridge was rejected.

3. After the War I had a most interesting conversation with an ex-Officer who had served in both the British and American armies. His father was an American and mother English, on the outbreak of the War, he was commissioned into the Rifle Brigade (Greenjackets) but on the USA coming into the War he transferred to their Army. In the original plan for Market Garden an American Airborne Division was to be dropped at Arnhem. When Montgomery went to see General Oma Bradley my informant was present as an Intelligence Officer. Bradley, put his finger on the map and said the American Division at Arnhem would be in great danger of being destroyed. On reflection Montgomery replaced the American Division with the 1st British Airborne Division. This was unfortunate as it broke a tidy

> organisation. The allotment of the Americans on a Corps basis to the capture of Nijmegen and the Arnhem bridges, and the 1st British Airborne Division to deal with most of the south up to Nijmegen.

We established ourselves just short of the railway line, with the enemy dug in of the far side of the embankment. D Coy, on our right, flank, came under fire and quickly occupied a large farm building and an orchard some 200 yards away.

A Coy, on the left, aggressively engaged the Germans with mortars and anti-tank guns before establishing itself in another farm 500 yards from the railway embankment.

Our patrols that night reported movements of tanks and other tracked vehicles in the area north east of Elst, which we understood to be strongly held by two battalions of SS Troops and about 20 tanks.

During September 24 and 25, I Worcestershire's and 7 Shropshire Light Infantry encountered fierce enemy opposition. But next morning, we were heartened somewhat by the news that two companies of Dorset's had succeeded in crossing the Needer Rijn.

The situation in our own sector was quiet, until about lunchtime, when Major Parker, spotted movement near the railway trucks just in front of D Coy's position.

He ordered an anti-tank gun to open fire . . . and we thought Armageddon was upon us! One of the trucks disappeared with an earth shattering roar . . . it obviously contained explosives. A young gunner officer on observation duties was blown from one room into another as the blast wrecked part of D Coys farm. He was knocked unconscious, although he recovered to pluckily continue with his duties. John Fry was wounded slightly so I brought him back to serve at battalion Headquarters.

That night, certain adjustments were made in our position near the level crossing. A section of machine guns of 8 Middlesex, under Lieut Mike O'Connor, was brought up to knock out enemy troops who were deeply dug in along the embankment near the river.

Although at first a little conservative about their use in such a forward role, the 'Diehards' agreed after a successful day's shooting that it had been very much worthwhile.

We bagged ourselves a bonus by picking up a German airman who literally dropped in on us by parachute after his plane had crashed in the battalion area. Good news continued to come in. We heard that some 2,000 airborne troops and 140 Dorset's had been evacuated from the north side of the river, and that Elst had finally been cleared by the rest of the brigade. We knew that a great deal of credit belonged to 5DCLI and 4/7th Dragoon Guards.

We continued to keep the lines of withdrawal open, despite some harassment by artillery and small arms fire. Several desperate attempts were made to counter attack the A Coy position. Small parties of German Marines came charging over the railway embankment, displaying a complete lack of fieldcraft. They met their inevitable fate at the hands of the now battle-hardened veterans of A Coy. But with our positions now well known to the enemy, we were under constant fire. It was now that we suffered one of our biggest personal blows in the whole campaign.

Major Parker, who had distinguished himself so conspicuously since I appointed him to lead our crack A Coy, was hit in the stomach by a splinter from an 88 shell which penetrated his command post in the company's farmhouse. He was seriously wounded; all I could do was to thank him for his services as he was evacuated by stretcher. The loss of this extraordinary man was a great one to the battalion. He came from a humble background . . . enlisting as a boy bugler in that famous regiment the Oxford and Buckinghamshire Light Infantry the 43rd of Foot.

Although 90% of my officers were from public school or grammar school backgrounds and were excellent men, Harry Parker, from a humbler background was outstanding. He was splendid in command in battle, aggressive but cool, and an excellent tactician, he really enjoyed battle. Happily he was to recover from his wounds and received an MC to accompany his MM. But he did not return to the battalion and was sent to an OCTU as an instructor before being invalided out of the Army.

Like David Willcocks, Harry was to carve a corner in music after the war, becoming leader of Birmingham Municipal Orchestra. With autumn fast approaching, the hot sultry weather gave way to chilling rain, a foretaste of the long, cold winter that was to come.

But the weather could not dampen our spirits when we heard in the early morning of September 27 that we were to be relieved by 5 Wilts and to move into a rest area.

Later in the day, recce parties of the relieving battalion arrived and it was agreed that a daylight takeover was practicable, as long as D Coy remained in position to provide cover.

A daylight relief operation would have the advantage of being much quicker and less fatiguing than a night one.

The operation began in late afternoon, and the skilled and disciplined movement of 5DCLI was difficult to spot. The men moved in dispersed formation, with an interval of 80 yards between each soldier. I was counting on sleepy and unobservant German look outs. There was no fire from the enemy on the high ground north of the river or from those over the railway line until the operation was nearly complete.

Then, some of the relieving troops, who were moving in normal formation of five yards between each man, in spite of being asked not to do some were spotted, and heavy mortar fire was brought down on C Coy. There were a few casualties, including Major Rucke Keene, company commander, who was wounded in the hand. Some years later I remembered this manoeuvre in Korea in 1951 and used it to surprise the Chinese in 'Operation Commando' and also it got the assaulting Australian – Scots companies off fresh after a nights rest under the noses of the enemy.

We arrived during the night at Andelst, a clean and well built Dutch village five miles west of Nijmegen, in time for a good meal and a well earned sleep.

Next day, we moved again to Oosterhoot, from where we had started our dash to Driel. Oosterhoot is a large village, surrounded by orchards, in the area Polden between Nijmegen and Arnhem which the Dutch have ingeniously transformed into a highly productive fruit growing centre.

Bordered by the Lower Rhine, to the north, and the Wall, which skirts Nijmegen, this bogland was known to us simply as 'the Island'. With 43 Div being withdrawn over the river south of Nijmegen, we of 5DCLI were to be left as the Island reserve battalion under 50 Div, which was sharing a defensive role with 101 US Airborne Div.

Infantry of the 43rd Division being inspected by Field Marshal Montgomery in Holland

Although the houses of Oosterhoot still showed evidence of the previous fighting, they provided us with comfortable enough accommodation, and we soon settled down to a steady routine existence of cleaning our weapons and equipment and getting ourselves back to parade ground smartness. Several carefree nights were spent in Battalion HQ Mess, a pleasant house jealously watched over by its owner with a great log fire burning in the lounge, while David Willcocks entertained us at the piano. It was here he composed his lovely melody *Oosterhoot, a song of Arnhem.*

As an army, we were now definitely on the defensive, and would have to wait for our supply lines to be shortened before we could resume our onward march.

But the Germans strongly resented our hold on the Island and Hitler gave orders for the elimination of what he regarded as a direct threat to the Reich. His first effort was to destroy the great bridges over the Rhine. German frogmen succeeded in blowing a big gap in the railway bridge, but their efforts against the road bridge failed.

Then, on October 1, the Germans counter-attacked in the Elst area with 9 and 116 Panzer divisions. We moved to a village called Bennel, into a lay-back position near the Green Howards, who had withstood heavy counter-attacks.

But the enemy had gained some ground and the losses on both sides had been considerable. I was sorry to hear that the Green Howards dead included the son of my old CO in Egypt – by now General Harold Franklyn, C-in-C Home Forces.

After a sleepless night awaiting further attacks, the good news came that the front held by 50 Div was stable and we moved back to the comparative comfort of Oosterhoot.

Though we were on two hours' notice to move, everyone managed to get a bath and a limited number of all ranks crossed the Waal to visit the clubs which had been organised in Nijmegen. But they were under orders to get back before dusk, when the Luftwaffe would sweep in to give the road bridge its nightly attention.

The only enemy vehicle we were pleased to see was a German bus, painted and converted into a PRI (?) wagon from which a cheerful and efficient sergeant named Hill would dispense cigarettes, chocolate and razor blades and all those other little commodities without which civilised man is at a loss.

CHAPTER SEVEN

Opheusden

Early in October, I was graced with a visit from the 30 Corps commander, General Horrocks. "George" he said, "I am placing 5DCLI under the command of General Maxwell Taylor's 101 Airborne Division. It is a great honour".

A great honour it might have been, but I could only reflect ruefully at the time that "bang goes four days rest out of the line!" As the American generals mobile reserve, were to move up in the support of 1st Bn, 506 Regt, who had been heavily counter-attacked from the west. We set up headquarter in a railway station near Andelst.

David Willcocks and I carried out our usual recce and found that the Americans' main strength was concentrated to the west, and the river line to the north was being watched by a thin screen only. We met the commander of 506 Parachute Regt, Col R.F. Sink, a forthright and charming Texan, and stayed for dinner. Seven years later, I was again to bump into him when, as a Lieutenant General, he was commanding 7th US Div in Korea.

The Americans were confident they could hold the position, and it was arranged that we sent Lieut Ritchie to them as liaison officer. Supported by tanks of the Scots Greys, the Americans had already given a good account of themselves. They had advanced on Opheusden, inflicting over 200 Casualties of the enemy at little cost to themselves. The battalion was on stand-by to move by the quick-lift method to any place necessary, and a number of concentration areas had been recced by myself and company commanders. It was while I was having lunch with three of my officers in the newly established officers' club in Nijmegen that Max Stock, my signals officer, entered with a worried look on his face.

"Colonel," he said, "the Germans are attacking the Americans and we are wanted for a counter attack!" We left the club smartly. Col Sinks' headquarters was established in a large house, with lots of glass windows. There seemed no suitable site for our Battalion HQ, except for some small houses alongside the Americans' house.

John Fry was with me and, to my amusement, began to sniff the air like a pointer dog. He then took out his entrenching tool and began to dig.

At the time, I thought the episode rather funny, but John my D Coy commander had foreseen trouble. Later in the day, we were glad to take shelter in the slit trenches that he had dug, as we were heavily shelled from the high ground to the east of the big river. The tough regular, who looked every inch the rugged farmer he was later to become in post war Bodmin, had led D Coy with conspicuous valour throughout the operations from Normandy to Holland. I though that John had enough and arranged for him to be posted as a G III officer to Division, where he continued to give his best.

His leadership and gallantry during the campaign were recognised by a much deserved MC. Throughout the rest of the war we felt that John Fry's heart was with the battalion borne out by the fact that he later became secretary of the DCLI Regimental Association.

Col Sinks men had been pushed back to the eastern edge of Opheusden. Under the command of 506 Regt combat group, we moved forward to a position about a mile of the east of the village.

The information was somewhat vague, but it appeared that a group of US troops were holding out in the area of the mill, while others, supported by the tanks of the Scots Greys, were guarding the road and railway area a couple of hundred yards east of the bridge.

One of the Scots Greys' tanks had already knocked out about 30 enemy troops, who were trying to move down the railway line, but the Germans, backed up by an anti-tank gun, had a firm hold on the area around the bridge. The Americans had little artillery of their own and our own team of gunners were engaged in hostilities elsewhere. But Sink and I decided that the best policy was a combined Anglo-American spoiling attack. The main thrust would be along the road leading to the village church, with the DCLI on the left and the Americans on the right, supported by a very thin artillery barrage and mortar fire.

An American company with a troop of Scots Greys, were to capture a small bridge and open up the road. Col Sink stressed that speed was vital, although I managed to gain an extra 30 minutes for preparation. The attack was fixed for 90 minutes from the completion of the conference. I gave out my orders. There was a confident air about our men as I briefly outlined the plan to B and D Companies, assembled in an orchard near the US command post. But it was apparent to us that this feeling was not shared by all the Americans.

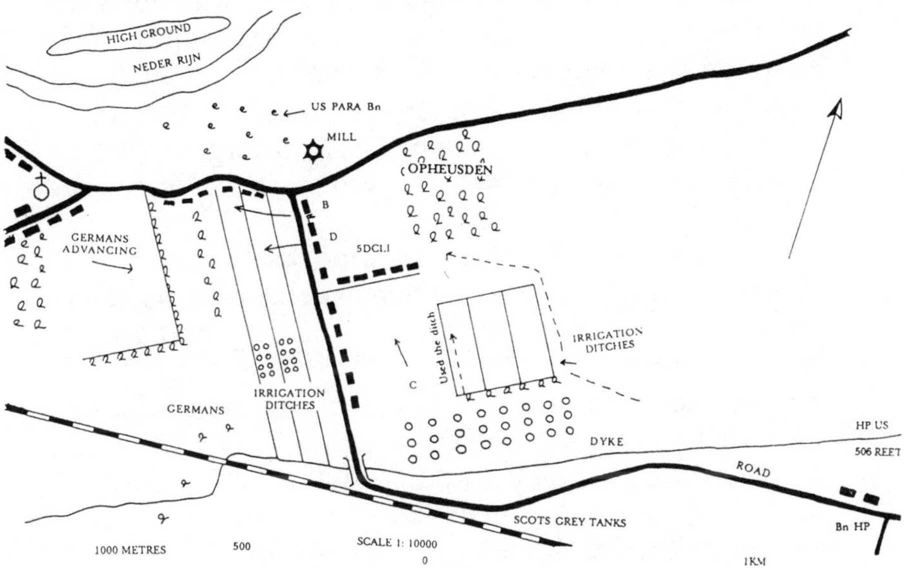

Brigadier General McAuliffe, the tough American hero of Bastogen, had sat in with us while I was giving out my orders. One sensed that he was not quite sure of his 'Limey' allies. On the other hand, Brigadier Peter Essame, who had arrived at the end of the order group, was clearly worried about what might happen to his DCLI, owing to the lack of artillery support.

Guided by an American officer who knew the ground, D Coy set off along a ditch that ran alongside the road, out of sight of any observers in the houses on the south side of the village.

It was while crouched in that evil-smelling, water filled ditch on the out skirts of an insignificant village in Holland that the carnage, suffering and misery being endured by the Allied troops suddenly had a meaning for Sgt E.J. Richards.

> "A touching and dramatic scene occurred that will for ever be imprinted on my mind," he was to write later. I was with the leading company with the company commander, Captain Spencer, and others of his HQ. "As I looked back along the curve of the dyke, I could see the long thin line of the whole battalion stretched out behind me. We lay there and sweated for a few moments and watched the road for any movement.
>
> All of a sudden, there struggled down the road from the direction of the shell-torn village a Dutch family fleeing to safety with their meagre belongings.
>
> To them, it must have seemed as if they were alone in this little part of the world, and as they got nearer to us we could see the anxiety and terror on their faces.
>
> They got within a few yards of us, not realising that British troops were so near. Then, as they crossed the road, they could see what I could see . . the long line of Cornwall's hidden from the enemy in the ditch.
>
> The change in their faces was a thing I'll never forget. A boy shouted to his parents that 'they are Tommies!' and the whole family stood still in the centre of the road heedless of the shells while tears of gratitude streamed down their faces.
>
> It was then that I reached the height of proudness that I was a British soldier of liberation!"

D Coy left the protection of the ditch and moved north across the first footbridge over the dyke and through a copse.

They came under heavy German artillery fire and the advance became somewhat disorganised. With his men delayed, Spencer finally pushed on with less than half the company. He reached the area of the mill and made contact with a US Major who had 150 men under his command.

As the barrage ended, Captain Spencer had to decide whether to press home the attack with his depleted force, or wait for the company to reorganise. He decided to err on the side of caution and wait.

He tried to contact Battalion HQ, but wireless communication failed. Finally, the rest of the company arrived. On a whistle signal from the Americans, both forces swept forward.

The Germans waited for them to cover the first 50 yards before opening fire with six light machine guns from a ditch about 80 yards from the road.

But their aim was wild, and D Coys two leading platoons, led by Sgt Baron and Lieut Snell, surged forward, firing from the hip and hurling grenades. The machine gunners were all killed or captured, and the Cornishmen swept on, knocking out two more posts. It was then that the enemy brought in their 88s and mortars.

The German riflemen, who were sited in depth and holding the line of the hedge in strength, joined in, and the casualties mounted among the two platoons.

But still they pushed on. Sgt Baron, MM, and Pte Smithson fell dead only a few yards from the hedge. Another stout hearted man defying the withering fire, set up his Piat and knocked out a machine gun behind the hedge. I was particularly saddened by the death of this most gallant sergeant. He had fallen in love with an attractive French girl on the Seine, and, to aid the romance, I had sent him on leave to marry her.

He had only just returned from his short honeymoon to take part in the battle.

Lieut Durden had by now moved up his reserve platoon. With Spencer and Snell both wounded, it was left to him to reorganise the shattered company and consolidate the position.

The wounded were collected and evacuated to the mill. It was to the Germans' credit that they observed the rules of war and did not fire while this was going on.

Eventually, Major Hingston, with just one platoon, arrived at the mill area, and made contact with Captain Spencer and the American Major, Spencer had been hit in the face and had lost a lot of blood. The mill was filled with British and American wounded.

But he could still think clearly and suggested to Hingston that B Coy attacked just south of the road towards the church. It seemed sound enough advice, and the Americans, despite their tiredness and losses, were game to try again.

I went forward down the road to see if I could get a better view, but could see nothing through the orchard. I therefore walked back to Sinks headquarters to agree with him a change of plan. To get there as quickly as possible, I used the road instead of the ditch running alongside. I did not endear myself to some US Pioneers busy restoring the culvert, as I immediately attracted the enemy shellfire from the high ground.

Major Hingston then began to reassemble his scattered company. It was here that the company runner, Private Bassett, was to distinguish himself so valiantly.

> "I had left him behind, a short way from the village, with orders to guide in the missing sections as they reached him," said Major Hingston. "Not content with leaving it at that, he returned four times across bullet swept ground to find, collect, and bring forward groups of the company until eventually the whole company was assembled in the village."

It was, the company commander added, a "very brave piece of work". This was not the only time Bassett was to display such courage, later in the campaign, he was promoted to CSM and earned himself the MM.

The combined attack started at 1600 hours. The first 200 yards of B Coy's thrust was unopposed, and Sgt Steele's 10

Platoon and Company headquarters were able to establish themselves in a big house.

While the Cornishmen were awaiting the signal from their American allies, two Germans strolled up as bold as brass, unaware of what had happened. They were speedily dealt with, but a third man was seen slipping away. He was obviously not long in making his report; within a short time the company found itself the subject of heavy mortar attack, which took a steady toll.

Then the combined Allied assault began in earnest. With the American commander on the right giving the order, B Company surged forward towards the German positions on an elevated piece of ground beyond the Orchard. Two sections of 10 platoon were badly mauled as they tried to work their way through the orchard. The rest of Sgt Steele's men moved through the gardens of a row of detached homes on the left.

They went cautiously from house to house, towards a big building at the end that would give them a good vantage point over the enemy positions. But the Germans obviously knew what was in their minds. As our men reached it, the house received a direct hit from a mortar shell and burst into flames, blocking their way and filling the air with blinding and choking smoke.

Undaunted, the platoon worked its way through the gardens of the house and engaged the enemy from 100 yards' range. Major Hingston then swung 11 Platoon round and all along the combined Anglo-American front a wild roar of small arms fire burst out. But even at this close range it was difficult to locate the foe, so effective was their concealment.

For L Cpl Howes, of Company HQ, it was like something out of an Errol Flynn war film. He said:

> "The Americans were impressing us with what appeared to both their pluck and their foolhardiness.
>
> They seemed to have no thought for personal safety and actually strolled from place to place. An American soldier would walk to the middle of the

> road, kneel on one knee, let off a burst or two from his automatic weapon and then walk back to cover.
>
> Of course, they were having plenty of casualties."

The spirit of the men of the 506 RCT is well illustrated by the conduct of one of them – badly wounded in the foot. When we tried to get him back on a stretcher he insisted that he could crawl back.

The Germans tried to move in an armoured SP gun, but after a few wild rounds it was driven off by our Bren and mortar fire. Hingston, in spite of a slight wound, was in good spirits. "I got the definite impression that things were going well and that we had won this scrap," he later wrote.

"The enemy fire was dying down and both we and our allies were still advancing and I felt that we would make the line of the church." Then a message came from the US Major to say that they had run out of ammunition. Hingston was asked to cover the American withdrawal and then drop back. The American automatic rifle could be wasteful in ammunition.

While all this was going on, C Coy was having its own problems. It had not followed the detour of the two leading companies, but had instead chosen to move along the western irrigation ditch. The company came under heavy fire from houses occupied by Germans who had moved round to cut in behind the Americans. Lieut Welsh was killed in a gallant effort to lead his men across the exposed ground between the ditch and houses.

Company losses were severe, and the men could make no further headway. But they put down enough fire with Brens, mortars and Piats to hold the enemy in a deadly stalemate.

The American attack using marching rifle fire on the small bridge would have opened up the road, but had failed. The leading tank of the Scots Greys had been knocked out by an anti-tank gun, and now the way was blocked. This meant that the troops in the mill area were still dependent on the road running along the bund as a line of communication.

With no protective screens along the river bank to the north, this posed a problem for us, with a considerable number of wounded to evacuate. But Lieut Birchenall, the Pioneer officer, provided the answer. All the battalion Jeeps were rounded up for medical service, and Birchenall led them to the mill via a back route. Despite overshooting the mark on one occasion and nearly ending up in enemy lines, he accomplished his mission successfully, and by late that night all our wounded American and British had been ferried out.

By then, it had been decided to relieve us and the Americans with a fresh US Battalion, who would dig in a new defensive position a little further to the east in an orchard which gave some cover from prying eyes of the enemy on the high ground over the river opposite Opheusden.

We remained long enough for them to get established. Before leaving for a rest area at Ewijk, over the Wall, we received a visit from Major General Maxwell Taylor just before nightfall. He thanked the DCLI for our efforts.

In an official letter to the General, Col Sink was to later say of the DCLIs part in the combined action:

> "These Troops attacked on schedule with vigour and determination under command of Lt-Col G Taylor in the face of withering enemy fire. Their courage and ability was an inspiration.
>
> The gallantry of the British officers and men was outstanding, and instilled in the men of 506 Parachute Infantry the highest regard for the fighting ability of the British Infantry."

The enemy counter attacking troops belonged to Von Zongen's 15 Army which had escaped across the Scheldt.

Opheusden had proved one of the most difficult actions that 5DCLI had to fight in the whole campaign. This was because:

The time allowed to mount the short spoiling-attack, owing to the situation, was extremely short.

The approach was under observed fire from high ground.

The situation was fluid, and the battle shifting, with the Germans still infiltrating forward when our attack went in.

Control was most difficult from the point of view of the battalion HQ, as the irrigation ditches prevented the use of a carrier or Jeep. Also the wireless sets were extremely erratic;

*We were without our usual artillery officer and had no forward observation officers and little artillery and was available from US artillery.

I was dissatisfied with myself having once launched the attack but then having so little influence on the chain of events . . . it was very much a company commanders battle in which they all did well. Moving back that night in my jeep I reflected sadly on the loss of good men like Welsh and Baron. It was a bright starlit night and looking up into the vast orb of the heavens that seemed so remote from our puny affairs.

Nevertheless, the battalion had fought stoutly and, by its quickly mounted spoiling attack and sturdy defence stablised the situation alongside the gallant American Paratroops and prevented a serious penetration of the front. Our casualties numbered 70 . . . mainly wounded . . . but we had inflicted at least equal losses on the enemy.

October and much of November was spent by 43 Division holding the front, along side the Americans on the eastern flank of the nijmegen salient. Failure at Arnhem had delayed Montgomery's plans to cross the Rhine and strike at the Ruhr. Now, the Allies had to take the inland port of Antwerp to shorten their supply lines, which still stretched back to Normandy.

Having recovered from the shock of Arnhem, the Germans had assembled strong forces to hold the Sheldt Estuary, by which the deep-water Belgian port Antwerp was aided by the strong defences of the Flushing area. The policy of 5DCLI during this time was active defence patrol raids, and harassing artillery fire, on a four-days-on, four-days-off routine. Much of our time out of contact with the enemy was taken up in training. We were in an area just to the west of the enemy held Reichswald Forest.

General Eisenhower, the Supreme Allied Commander, had directed that the enemy be given no chance to reorganise in the West during the winter of 1944, and therefore the offensive should be maintained unceasingly along the whole Allied front from Basle to Antwerp.

His objective was to bring the whole of the Allied Armies up to the line of the Rhine. General Horrocks' 30 Corps, of which 43 Div formed part was to work on the extreme right flank of 21 Army Group and capture Geilenkirchen, to enable the US 9th Army to push through to Linnich.

In mid-November, intensive planning and training began for "Operation Clipper", which was to start on the 18th of the month. Geilenkirchen was to be enveloped by encircling attacks from the north west and south east delivered by 43 Div and 84 US Div respectively.

The Wessex objectives were a cluster of well built German villages in flat, featureless country dotted with large woods, which would seal off Geilenkirchen from the east.

The whole area was overlooked by high ground on the east of the River Wurm, on which part of the formidable Siegfried Line stood, which was the objective of the American 84th Division.

The 84th Division had just arrived from the States and were a new formation . . . from what I saw briefly of their training they looked excellent troops. Horrocks was determined to help them as he knew that their first battle would be a difficult and tough one so put the battle experienced Sherwood Rangers Armoured Regt of our Army under their command though they had tanks of their own also some detachments of that unique British Division the

79th, with what they called their funnies: flails (that could beat a path through a mine field) and flame tanks, petard tanks that could hit a pill box with a flying dust bin full of explosive and also our Corps Artillery. With the Guards Armoured Division in reserve and our Division supported by the 8th Armoured Brigade and the American 84th Division made up his Corps.

I was asked by the Brigadier to go across to see the CO of the American battalion on our immediate right. I saw their Colonel, his name was Gomez, a short alert dark haired man, we fixed up various points of contact and co-operation including the use of Yellow smoke, to show our progress in the advance, it was his first battle. As I was leaving him having wished him good fortune, I made a throw away remark saying "don't put all your goods in the shop window". He quickly responded and asked me what I meant, therefore without being patronizing (he was many years my junior) I was able to advocate the use of depth in the attack, we had a thorough discussion. I heard later that his battalion fought a very successful battle, years later he became a General.

The Cornish battalion would attack Hocheide, which would take us on a flank march right across the face of the guns defending the German border. We could only hope that the enemy on the high ground would be too busy dealing with the American attack on Prummern to bother with us.

Planning was carried out meticulously and briefing was done on an excellent cloth model, with the aid of maps and air photos.

At 0830 hours on November 18, the battalion crossed the border into Germany an historic occasion for both us and the brigade. Previously only patrols had entered into the stronghold of the Third Reich. Now we were part of the first British attack on German soil.

I reminded the men of this as they moved down the road into the forest where our assembly area was located, just south of the Gangelt-Gillrah road.

The Royal Engineers had cut out rough tracks, elevated in

status with such grand names as Bond Street, Regent Street and The Strand. The atmosphere was light hearted as we dug ourselves into the sandy soil and had a meal. Pounding of the enemy positions by over 400 pieces of artillery and rocket-launching Typhoon aircraft had started early that morning.

At about 1130, the brigade began moving to the start line, led by 7 Somerset Light Infantry, who were to capture Niederheide. We were given 2½ hours to pass through them, to be ready to launch our attack by 1500 hours, just about the minimum time such an operation could be carried out in war.

We were on the move by the time the Somerset's went in. The column was moving in fits and starts on the only approach road. I went forward on the back of a motorbike to see the situation for myself. Up ahead, I came across the cause of the delay . . . the many tanks supporting the attack had become bogged down in the soft ground; the road was cluttered with the carriers, anti tank guns and jeeps of the Somerset's and Worcester's.

Time was slipping away in giant strides, and it was necessary to force our way through this jam if we were to keep to our tight schedule. I used a megaphone to good effect, and soon our leading D Coy was approaching Niederheide, where fighting was still going on. Large groups of Germans, stunned by the relentless artillery support, had surrendered in droves.

Sgt Thorpe, our Intelligence NCO, was directed to meet D Coy and guide them to the start line. David Willcocks and I then pushed on through the village with the leading troop of tanks.

Some of the tanks became trapped in the treacherous mud, fretting frantically as they churned their way free. From the middle of the road which was the start line, we could see Major Lonsdale with D Coy's leading platoon moving up through the swirling mist and smoke of the artillery barrage.

Lieut John Rabet's reserve platoon were lying just in front of the road, waiting tensely for the signal to move forward.

BATTLE FOR HOVEN NOVEMBER 1944

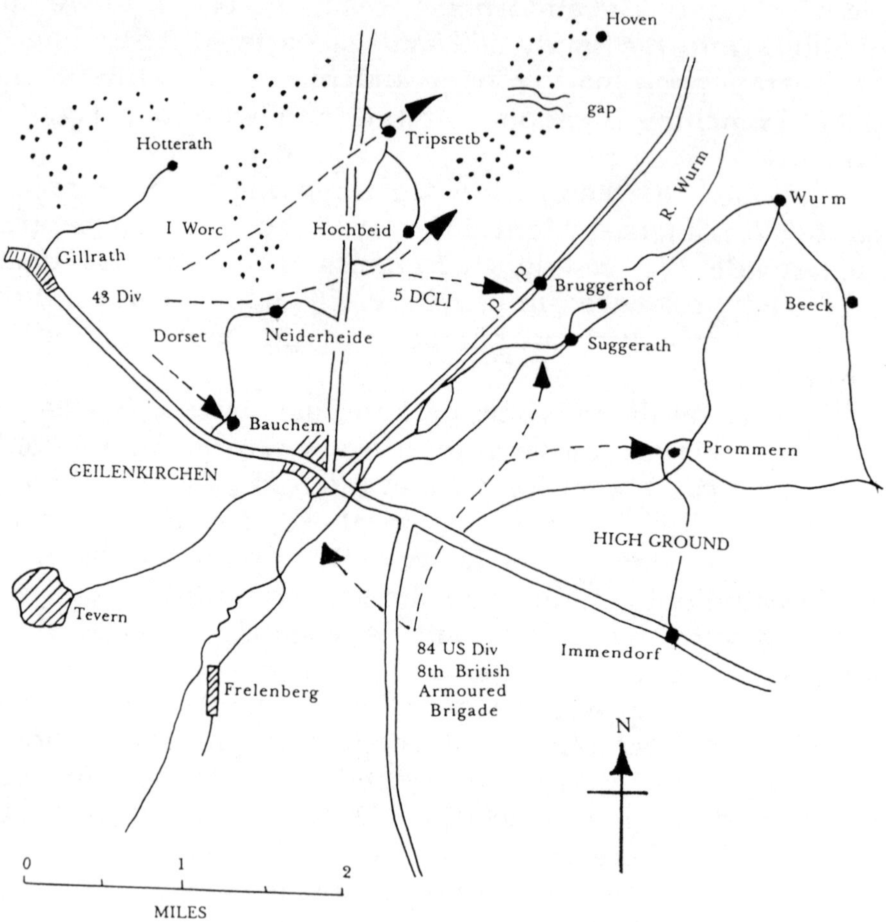

Tanks of the 4/7 Dragoon Guards roared through at great speed to support the D Coy onslaught; emerging cautiously from the wood in open order now were B Coy, making their way to my command post on the road.

I again made good use of the megaphone for the maintaining of direction and momentum.

All this activity had stirred the enemy into savage reaction. Heavy shells whined overhead and pitched crashingly into the wood among the Worcester's. Then the range shortened, and the black ugly bursts began to appear along the hedge near the road, where a line of Khaki figures were moving. The shelling was intensive and accurate, and the line suddenly broke for the open in bid to sidestep this horror of bursting explosive steel.

They turned out to be HQ of 1 Worcester's. Their CO, Lieut Col R.E. Osborne Smith, who had led the battalion so ably for most of the campaign, was among the wounded.

Meanwhile, the Cornwall's D Coy were sweeping forward with great dash and the leading platoons soon over came the resistance offered by defensive posts south west of the village. Ten prisoners were taken.

Rabet's platoon, however, suffered casualties through mortar and sniper fire from the left flank.

The tanks moved in to engage these positions. After a brief recce by Major Lonsdale, 18 platoon, covered by the fire of the 7 Platoon entered the neck of the wood and encountered little resistance. The enemy had fled.

Hochiede was now ours, but holding on to it would be another matter. A track from the village ran all the way down to main road. Advancing down this track D Company under Major Holland occupied a small copse. I added an Anti tank gun and a Vicker Machine gun to the trap after I had been round to see Holland; we had cut the main road running north east from Geilenkirchen. The first 150 yards passed through a narrow gorge, with steep banks and trees on each side.

The main German force had no idea their road had been cut, and at about 1800 hours one of their platoons was seen marching in threes on their way to Geilenkirchen. D Coys light machine guns opened up on them. Seven of the enemy fell dead and four were taken prisoner. The rest scattered.

They proved to be from 104 Panzer Grenadiers.

We feared that the incident would alert the enemy to our presence, and the next few hours were spent digging in and improving our defences as best as possible in the dark.

Mines were laid in the road and covered with leaves and twigs. Unfortunately they were put down in pairs, and this was later to prove insufficient. Our trap accounted for two horse-drawn ammunition carts and most members of an exploratory enemy platoon. But the big prize . . . a Tiger tank . . . came through at 3 o'clock in the morning, obviously heading for Kraudorf.

It hit the mines and stopped. The crew, except for the driver, jumped out and proceeded to clear the remaining explosives. But a few bursts of a light machine gun put paid to their efforts. The tank drove on, seemingly unperturbed. The grenades were not sufficient to break it's tracks.

The November dawn broke to low clouds and continuous drizzle. The weather matched the men's mood . . . they had not eaten a hot meal since breakfast two days before. With the battalion's transport bogged down near Hocheide, there was little likelihood of getting any supplies through until nightfall.

On the lighter side, A Coy's ranks had been swelled by two unexpected newcomers . . . the two horses from the ill-fated ammunition wagons of the previous night's exploits. They grazed contentedly in a field behind company lines, expertly dodging the mortar and artillery concentration that fell about them from both sides.

Spirits sank lower when news came through that the American attack on Geilekirchen had been postponed for 24 hours. It would mean another long night spent in isolation.

But with the darkness came the company carriers, and the CQMS with hot food and rum. Things did not seem so bad after all!

The morning of the 20th was spent cleaning weapons and resting as much as possible while D Coy waited for the Americans to press home their attack.

Then in the early afternoon, things began to happen. First, a few German troops were seen approaching the company's positions from the direction of Geilenkirchen. Gradually, the numbers increased, and it became apparent that about 40 of them had worked their way into the wood and were trying to break through 17 platoon's defences.

The platoon responded with vigour, but then 8 platoon reported enemy penetrated through the wood towards them, and No 9 found their attention occupied by three menacing SP guns.

By now, every conceivable weapon was firing in all directions; it was obvious that the Germans were determined to carve themselves out an escape route from Geilenkirchen.

Fortunately, the company wireless set was still working, despite the fact that the top aerial had been shot away, and Ptes Reynolds and Potter did well to alert Battalion HQ of the situation.

Soon, the surrounding woods were being swept by machine guns of the 4/7 Dragoon Guards, 3 inch mortars, and artillery fire. C Coy were at the ready to launch an immediate counter-attack; everything possible was done to relieve the besieged D Coy.

The battle raged for 45 minutes, and for a time it was touch and go. An enemy tank, with a following of infantry, penetrated the centre of the position and neutralised an anti-tank crew. But the Cornwall's . . . experienced veterans of many battles with German armour . . . poured small arms fire into the gargantuan and blinded its crew with smoke grenades. The tank turned tail and fled.

Lieut Williams' 8 Platoon were inflicting heavy casualties on their section of the enemy, often in close quarter fighting. 9 Platoon were busy accounting for the SP guns and crews, and No. 8 Platoon sandwiched their attackers between themselves and the Americans, who had by now made an appearance.

Cpl Lynch, with great gallantry, ran over open ground, defying enemy fire, to contact them. His was a story of great interest. During the battle of Hill 112, shocked and exhausted by his terrible experiences, this young soldier then a private had deserted.

After being found in Baycux, he was brought before me. His honest manner and open face resulted in my giving him a second chance, instead of putting him up for court martial. In the subsequent fighting, Lynch quickly rose to the rank of corporal. In the Hoven action still to come, he led his men in a counter-attack, accounting for many of the enemy with his Bren, until a bullet shattered his arm.

He stoutly refused to be evacuated and continued fighting until a considerable time later. We were unable to get a decoration for this gallant NCO, which was so often the case. I firmly believe that the Brigadier or Divisional Commander should be given an allotment of awards for other ranks and that all ranks should wear on their shirt sleeve a coloured stripe if they have fought in five actions in the teeth arms.

So, we had successfully linked up with the Americans. But the Dorset's were fighting a violent action in the clearing of a wood to the west of Tripsnah; it was later to become known as Dorset Wood.

The US assault up the Wurm Valley was meetig fierce resistance after initial success. Blazing British tanks of the Sherwood Rangers, who were supporting the Americans along the Siegfried Line, could be seen from our positions.

Lieut Miles, one of our fine young officers, was killed by a direct hit on his slit trench, and Lieut Durden was slightly wounded during the intensive shelling of our positions in the southern edge of Hochied Wood. I immediately took steps to reduce the number of platoons in it. Otherwise 5DCLI had got off lightly in the battle to support the taking of Geilenkirchen. Our casualty toll had been one killed, four wounded. At least 21 Germans were dead, and nine wounded. And their three SP guns had been knocked out. No doubt they had considerably more casualties.

CHAPTER EIGHT

Cornwall Wood

Oh grim Wood of Hoven
Now mined and silent lying
Here men of Cornwall fought and died

On the morning of November 21, we received a 'warning order' from Brigade that we have to capture Hoven, a hamlet on the northern edge of Hocheid Wood, and then take the village of Kraudorf, on its right.

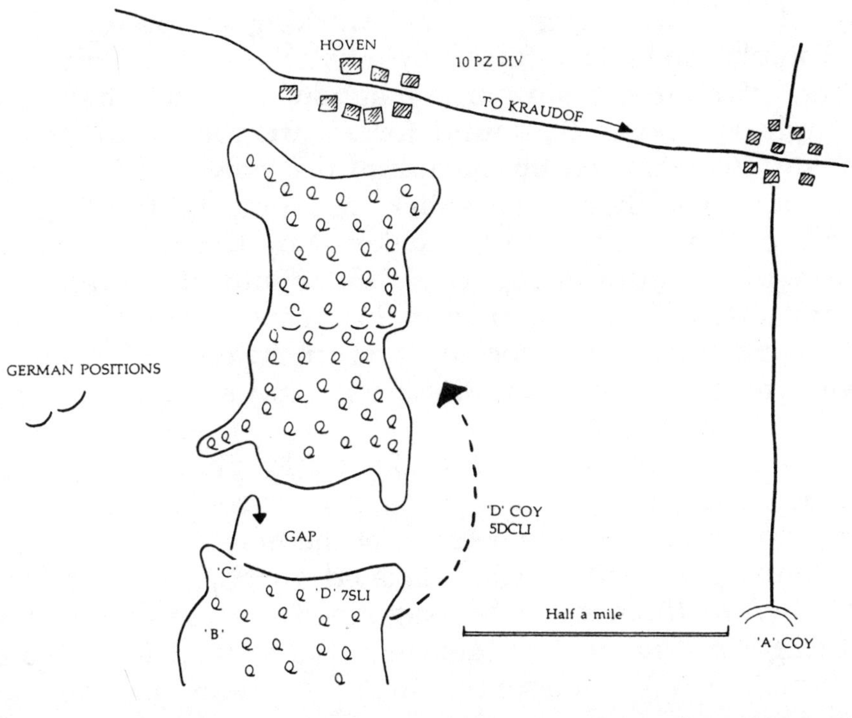

This would push the enemy farther east, and eliminate the attention of their big guns firing on Geilenkirchen, which was a bottle-neck of the lines of communication and supply of the 9th US Army, who were fighting farther the south in the Hurgtgen Forest in one of the most bitter battles of the war.

I at once went forward with David Willcocks to have a good look at the ground. We reached the edge of the Wood opposite what was to become known as 'the Gap'; it was held by a company of 7 Somerset Light Infantry.

Protected by the remaining leaves of late autumn on the trees, we surveyed the scene across the Gap; it was a depressing sight. Everywhere lay the shattered debris of war. But something of a more sinister nature was bothering me... all my training and instincts warned me that this operation was unsound.

The reasons were clear to me: a tired and under strength battalion, after a period of sustained action, was not in fit state to launch another attack. The rifle companies, except for C Coy, were down to about 60 men, instead of 100 – the arrival of reinforcement was not working smoothly.

The plan for attack for a single battalion on the divisional front, without the supporting actions of other battalions, though it is tactically sound for a battalion to attack on a narrow front backed by maximum fire power, it is essential that other battalions also attack to widen the frontage in a series of blows, this can be achieved by timed switching of the artillery supporting fire. We would doubtless meet heavy fire and be forced to endure severe counter attacks. We were likely to especially endure heavy defensive fire from the bastions of the Siegfried Line sited on the high ground to our right.

It was doubtful if our tanks could give us close fire support; also certainly, no anti-tank guns could be sent up or tanks to either objective because of the mud.

Standing in a slit trench, I dictated my objections to David, who wrote them on a message pad and despatched the message to Brigade Headquarters. We arrived for Brigadier Essame's conference preceding the attack in the early afternoon, and were astonished to discover that it was being held in a large brown marquee with no attempt at concealment, which showed the confidence our army had in our air superiority. Though the November weather precluded its use.

The latest information was that the enemy were holding a

line of posts some 300 yards back from the gap. But I thought that they might have come forward to the gap.

The brigadier was perturbed at my message; it was the first time I had shown opposition to his plans or orders. He took me by the arm, and we walked up and down the big tent. "George" he said kindly, "I am not asking your battalion to attack on its own. The Americans on the high ground will attack simultaneously in the direction of Wurm". That being the case, I felt I could object no longer.

It had been decided that to confirm the information about the enemy positions in the wood, the Scout Platoon would send out a special night patrol. The brigade fire plan envisaged a preliminary night-long bombardment on the wood to soften up the enemy. We had a good system that David would take down the first part of the Brigadiers orders and send it back by dispatch rider to battalion headquarters this enabled the battalion to start to prepare for operations. This information was sent back to battalion, where my second in command, Andy Martin, decided after discussion with Bill Gorman, the adjutant, to cancel the special patrol because of the danger to them. It was a case of Murphy's Law.

For meanwhile, at the brigadier's discussion group, I pointed out that a night bombardment would rob our troops of much needed sleep and probably give away any chance we had of surprise. So the artillery barrage was switched to the Straeten area, with the idea of bluffing the Germans we were going there. Artillery support for the DCLI attack was to take the form of a block barrage, starting 250 yards away from the edge of the wood. It was feared that, to put it any nearer our troops, shells hitting the trees might cause casualties among the leading platoons.

To bridge the gap and secure a start line for us, 7 Somerset's Company would shoot us into the edge of the Wood with Brens, 2 in mortars and Piats, in case the enemy had moved some of their posts forward to cover the gap.

The battalion plan was for C Coy, the fresher one, to attack and secure the wood; B Coy would then leap-frog through and capture Hoven. D Coy, moving in the slip-stream of this attack, would move on Kraudorf.

This was timed so that the wood would clear of Germans, thus eliminating the danger of interference from this flank. As a further precaution, smoke was to be used to cover D Coy.

As A Coy could not be relieved from their holding role at Bruggnhof, the company of Somerset's would take their place. A tank squadron of 4/7 Dragoon Guards would neutralise the left and right edges of the wood and then move forward to support the attacks on Hoven and Kraudorf, if possible if mud would allow. The open ground between the two places would be swept by machine guns of the Middlesex Regiment.

I decided that each company would be led by their respective seconds in command, so that the commanders could be ensured a good night's sleep; I knew they would need to be fresh to meet the German counter attack which could constitute the crisis point of the battle, so they went back to the transport lines 'B' Echelor.

In the case of D Coy, I intended to use an officer who had distinguished himself by his bravery in Normandy. But I had kept him in reserve too long, giving him too much time to dwell on things, thus undermining his morale.

This was my fault; I should have brought him back to the front line before deciding to use him in such a crucial role. It taught me to rest officers and NCOs when possible, but not for long periods. The battle was to be run from two command positions . . . advanced and main. The former constituted a number of slit trenches dug by our pioneers in a small clearing about 40 yards short of the start line. It would be manned by myself, David Willcocks, Tom Brewis, the RA battery commander, and my signals officer. It was selected in this little clearing to avoid the danger of shells bursting in trees. The main HQ, in the cellar at Hochheid, would be operated by Andy Martin, Bill Gorman, and the commanders of HQ and support companies all excellent soldiers. Before moving to my command post, I spoke to some of the men who would be leading the attack. Just before the attack two enemy deserters were brought in. We were concerned to find they belonged to the reconnaissance regiment of a crack Panzer division our old enemy, but the news was too late for us to alter our plans.

We had believed that we were only up against one of Hitler's newly formed Folk Grenadier Divisions, but now it was our old enemy the 10th SS Panzer Division. That night before the attack because part of the battalion was holding a defensive position and could not be regrouped for orders, the Intelligence section produced for every rifle section a diagrammatic sketch of our plan. With the green and khaki of their uniform smocks blending with the fast decaying russet foliage of late autumn, the men of the DCLI began to advance to their start line area. Nothing could be heard but the crack of a twig under a clumsy boot and the steady creek of equipment. The men looked tense but confident. Then came the reassuring sight of our artillery passing high over the trees, followed by the loud crashing bangs as they found their targets. So far, so good.

C Company passed beyond the friendly cover of the foliage. Then, suddenly, the startling and maddening BRRRRRRRRP of the enemy's machine guns. Swelling to a crescendo, dominated by the frantic scything of the Spandaus, they had come forward to the gap. Our men were pinned down by this deadly hail, just ahead of the attack start line. The answering fire of the tired and depleted Somerset Light Infantry was insufficient to subdue the numerous hostile light machine guns that had been placed with calculated efficiency along the edge of the wood covering the gap.

Then the German artillery, mortars and 88s joined in, pummelling the area around our command post. Some shells and mortar bombs went off in ugly and not always effective bursts in the sodden ground . . . others, more deadly, burst in the trees.

It was this fire that caught the C Coy reserve platoon and destroyed it in seconds. The two leading platoons were trying to fight their way forward, and the left hand one, under Lieut Gay, managed to overcome a number of posts their but could not hold on. The right hand platoon were pinned down. Lieut Charles Davies, an experienced soldier of the

8th Army, was wounded in the head and arm and made his way back to the command post, swearing lustily against the Boche.

Major Kitchen, who had been having a night's rest, was with me in the command post. I sent him to take over command of his company. Kitchen was to report later "The situation did not look healthy; 15 platoon had ceased to exist. Moving with difficulty, I reached 14 platoon. They had suffered considerably. All this time we were being heavily mortared. In fact, neither before nor since have I experienced such an intensity of fire. I decided the company had shot its bolt as an attacking force and all we could do was to hold and fire back. It was a real shooting match . . . Bren v Spandau . . . and we gave as good as we got!

It was obvious our attack had failed. But a battalion like 5DCLI was not easily deterred. We would not accept defeat, angrily and tensely, I devised a fresh plan, concentrating my mind on the problem.

D Company, formed up and waiting on the right, we told not to attack Kraudorf, but to perform a slight right hook and move into the wood, covered by a barrage and smoke-screen, and then on to Hoven. Meanwhile C and B Companies and Carrier Platoon were, it seemed, winning fire superiority over the enemy. Gradually, the Spandaus became less active but the enemy mortars and artillery were maintaining fire with great regularity and precision.

The command post was a miserable affair, offering little cover. Owing to the tough tree roots, the slit trench in which it was established was only waste high. One shell killed my signaller, who was standing close to me, and the blast of another knocked me off my feet. I felt like a boxer who had been floored in the ring, desperately trying to get up to fight on. But I knew I could trust all ranks to fight to the bitter end. Under the new plan, D Company under the command of Captain Spencer was to capture Hoven. Their line of approach was to be the open ground to the right of the wood. they would be covered by a smoke screen; once in the wood they would be supported by an artillery barrage. The plan worked. They swept into the centre of the wood swiftly overcoming all enemy resistance, and soon on a two platoon front reached the edge of the wood near Hoven. The last stage of the attack took the form of a pincer movement. The right hand platoon soon reached it's objective of a large house; the left hand assault, under Lieut Savory, ran into heavy fire from hidden riflemen and men fell, killed or wounded.

Spencer then committed his reserves, under Sgt Williams, on the right flank. After further fighting, the hamlet was now firmly in our hands, along with 40 prisoners, as darkness fell. It was just before this that things began to go badly wrong. The Somerset Light Infantry, who were to move up in support, lost their way towards the wood confused by smoke, while dodging heavy artillery fire and ran into more of those deadly machine guns in the gap.

It was some time before we realised that the Somerset's move had failed. This meant that the DCLI D Company in Hoven were isolated.

Darkness meant new dangers at our little command post, a voice raised above a whisper would bring down a hail of fiery Spandau bullets from across the gap. There was much to be done; communications must be established with the men in Hoven; the wounded would have to be evacuated; food and arms were vital if D Company were to consolidate their position; if possible, we had to move the tanks up, but mud proved this impossible.

Who of us at the command post will forget that night as we strove to restore the orderly functioning of the battalion's machinery and carry out these tasks? I was in constant demand to make decisions.

It was about this time we had just received the news of successful assault on Hoven over the radio that the Brigadier had made his way up on foot and was given the good news. The brigadier relates: Despite the large number of wounded being evacuated, the high spirit of all ranks left a vivid impression on him, he wrote later on. "Lt Colonel Taylor, Captain Willcocks, his intelligence officer and Major Brewis, his Gunner, might well have been at a rugger match at Twickenham rather than fighting a sanguinary battle at close quarters with a Panzer Grenadier Regiment, in a filthy German wood on a damp November afternoon."

In reality it was a terrible time for us all, I asked him to give me back my A Company. Our wounded were a very grave problem. Fortunately we had used a new draft of some 30 reinforcement to help our stretcher bearers in a Roman chain back to the Regimental Aid Post, otherwise many would have died during the bitter November night. I decided to send a patrol into Hoven and with it went Cpl Adams of the intelligence section. Who could ever forget that one quiet question when I asked him to bring back a sketch of the companies positions and their defensive artillery fire plan . . . what colour should I use for the sketch, Sir? A very brave little man. The redoubtable Adams was later to retrace his route, and guide a small party of the Dorset Regiment sent up by Divisional headquarters, carrying much needed food, hot drinks, rum and ammunition to Hoven.

The patrol gallantly led by Cpl Adams managed to slip between the enemy posts by moving in the open ground to the east of the wood and returned to report the situation of the beleaguered garrison. From time to time enemy machine guns across the 'gap' opened fire on us. We were covered in mud and soaked to the skin with the piercingly cold November rain. Men trembled as if suffering from a violent ague.

Our maps were sodden and mud encrusted; lights could only be used by crouching at the bottom of muddy fox holes. The radio set that had worked so well had now, with much constant use, become tired and erratic. We had little time to make a decision. We had to take calm stock of the situation and all the time, the piteous cries of the wounded as we laboured to succour them were adding to the misery of that terrible night.

The battalion, battered and shaken, was like some virile giant beset and wounded, shaking himself free striving to overcome it's enemies. I sent Lieut Birchenall back to Brigade HQ with a request that 5DCLI should either be reinforced or withdrawn. On his arrival there, Bill

Birchenall met General Horrocks, the Corps Commander, who had motored through the night in pouring rain to see Brigadier Essame.

The General was aware of the great danger that now threatened the Cornwall's, without anti tank guns, stuck out nearly two miles ahead of the Americans on the high ground to our right.

The new United States Division the 84th (The Railsplitters) had fought their way into Gielenkichen and captured it. To start with in this battle they were opposed by one of Hitler's hastily raised 'Folk Grenadier Divisions? They were no match for the well trained, vigorous Americans. But the enemy was well supported by artillery and mortar fire from the Bastions of the Siegfried Line. Also machine guns well sited in concrete pill boxes and anti tank guns protected by mine fields barb wire and dragons teeth, proved a formidable system of defence – so it proved to be no walk over for the brave Americans.

Mud and the wet cold weather was a big factor, the former hindering the efforts of the tanks of the British Yeomanry (Sherman Rangers) to give close fire support on some occasions, though these veteran troops were a considerable help to the American Infantry.

Mud also made difficulties for the detachments of armoured vehicles of the British 79 Division with their collection of 'funnies'. Mud and anti tank guns took their toll on these skilled and courageous veterans.

After the capture of Gielenkirchen and Prummen and fighting their way down the Wurm valley towards Beck, resistance stiffened. The 9th Panzer Division had arrived, but the 84th persisted though progress was slower. A factor that militated against a quicker advance was lack of hot food and the forward troops had to rely on 'K' (cold) rations. Boots were also giving trouble; they did not keep feet warm and dry – hence 500 cases of trench foot. Nevertheless Linden fell to a workmanlike attack and shortly afterwards Beck was captured.

Under the command of Brigadier General Bollig under very difficult conditions this gallant Division had certainly won it's spurs.

Horrocks told Essame that he could withdraw 5DCLI if he thought fit. The brigadier argued that we had captured Hoven at great sacrifice and to pull us back now would be bad for morale. The corps commander then left him to try to get the Americans to push home an attack on our right. Essame told Birchenall that we were to hold on, but would be relieved some time next morning by the Wiltshire's.

I had the feeling that the brigadier's visit to the battalion the previous afternoon had clouded his judgement into thinking that the DCLI could do anything; the truth was, we just did not have the tools to complete the job. I would emphasise that he was an excellent Brigadier.

No tanks or anti-tank guns could be moved forward because of the mud, and we were therefore dependent on the short range piat or the indirect fire of the artillery.

Meanwhile, a chain of platoon posts were to be established along the eastern side of the wood to open communications and to protect the rear of the isolated Hoven garrison as soon as possible.

By 4 am, this force A Company, of some 90 men, under Major Kitchen, with Major Holland as 2 i/c, reached the wood and were dispersed into their respective positions. (Platoons in depth)

The isolation felt by these men in an exposed position was later summed up by Major Kitchen: "No sooner had we started to dig in, that a red very light went up in Hoven, followed by mortar fire. This was most perplexing, as we were under the impression that D Company was holding the part of the village which looked as it was held by the Boche. We could get nothing through on our wireless, and we felt very much out in the blue. (In actual fact, enemy patrols had been in the wood and located some of our positions.)"

Kitchen's feeling of loneliness was nothing compared with that of the men holding on to their slender foothold in Hoven. In some cases, the foe were only 30 yards away.

Just before dawn, a party of Germans reached the company HQ buildings and were dispersed following a sharp action. But not before the company wireless set their vital link with the battalion was damaged by the blast from a grenade.

To add to the desolation, the telephone line was cut. The dawn did little to alleviate the men's anxiety. In the dim first light of day, large numbers of enemy infantry later revealed as the 10th SS Division were seen moving up the hedgerows.

The defenders scythed into them with deadly Bren and rifle fire, but the SS men doggedly re-formed, this time supported by tanks. A well directed Piat bomb put one of these out of action, and the rest, for a time, kept warily out of range. There broad tracks enables them to move over the sodden ground – they also had the use of a road. Reinforcing the enemy attack were SP guns, which sent shells crashing into buildings, setting them alight.

Inside Company Headquarters, pandemonium reigned; wounded from both sides were everywhere. With the deafening sounds of battle stunning their senses, the signallers worked frantically to get the precious wireless working so that the command post could be informed of the company's predicament and use our own artillery to relieve the situation.

Strangely, by some topographical freak, we at the battalion command post could hear no sound of the desperate fighting through the rain drenched thickly wooded approach to the village.

Meanwhile, the battle was reaching a crisis point. Ammunition was running perilously low, and the rapidly dwindling band of survivors were using every grenade and bullet they could lay their hands on to keep the attackers at bay.

Weapons of fallen comrades were hastily brought back into the fight, then the ammunition and arms of German casualties and prisoners. Any slackening in the defensive fire brought the besieging infantry and tanks ever closer.

The company second-in-command, Captain Spencer, was told of an enemy tank approaching down the street. He said:

> "I at once ran upstairs with a Piat. The tank was now only 20 yards away. I leaned the Piat against

> the window-sill, took aim . . . and fired. It was a misfire.
>
> The tank crew, seeing this movement, swung their gun in my direction. There was a great flash, and I was temporarily blinded. Hit in the head, arm and leg, I crawled down into the cellar."

For the few survivors of D Company there remained one choice: surrender or retreat.

Major Lonsdale, he had been having a good nights sleep at B Echelor, but went forward to command his company. I as mentioned had foreseen that my company commanders having already been in action for many hours, must be rested, forseeing that a crisis would probably arise after we had captured Hoven. After handing over to their 2nd in commands I sent them back to the Transport Lines. Lonsdale decided to fight his way out.

With the remaining 15 or so fighting men, plus any walking wounded willing enough to try, they made a dash for it through a hole in a barn conveniently made for them by an enemy shell.

Adding to their one piece of good fortune, smoke from the blazing building blanketed their escape from the eyes of the avenging enemy. Things had been no quieter for Major Kitchen, with his small force behind Hoven. Following the discovery of their positions, the Germans laid down mortar fire.Said Kitchen:

> "We were holding all right, when we heard voices coming from the open country in the direction of Kraudorf. Holly (Major Holland) and I went to the edge of the wood to have a look. To our horror, we saw advancing in the uncertain light just before dawn above 60 Boche, advancing steadily towards us, talking at the tops of their voices. We held our fire until they were close, and then let them have it! They were completely surprised, and we inflicted many casualties."

Some of the Germans advanced bravely into the wood, and were engaged in close quarter fighting. Holland himself fought a successful 'duel' with a German at 12 yards range with his revolver. But then the enemy moved up two SP guns on the left, and started to pepper the wood with 88s. Major Holland, on his way back from organising a counter attack, was wounded by one of these shells. Added Kitchen: "When I heard about this, I felt very much alone". The situation was becoming desperate, with the Germans closing in from the front and from the left. "But our chaps were magnificent," said Kitchen. "I well remember Pte Everitt, my batman, killing four of the enemy with his Sten gun at 20 yards range. His was by no means the only brilliant effort." Just when things seemed to be at their worst, help arrived in the form of a platoon led by Lieut Williams. With great dash, they drove the attackers back which illustrated the great value of an immediate counter attack. "Then our wireless started to work, and I began to feel a bit better about things," remembered Kitchen.

But his optimism was short-lived. A stray bullet in the right shoulder put him out of action, and Lieut Williams took command. After receiving orders to withdraw, he fought a successful reguard action, getting all the survivors back safely.

Only when Major Lonsdale and his party arrived back from the shattered village of Hoven did the grim reality sink in: 5DCLI had suffered what was to be their only failure in many actions during my tenure of command 1944/5. I ordered Williams to withdraw which he skilfully did. By now we had got our artillery into action on to likely targets.

The only prisoners to fall into enemy hands were the wounded we had been forced to leave behind. They included the gallant Captain Spencer. Two of our stretcher bearers who remained with the wounded reported after the war that they had spent a whole day picking up German casualties. The Germans . . . soldiers of the formidable SS . . . had treated the prisoners with every kindness and had expressed great admiration for the strong fight our men had put up.

From a technical point of view, I put the failure to hold

Hoven down mainly to:

> The general fatigue of the men and the battalion machine before the action. We had already been engaged for over 96 hours.
>
> The heavy rain which turned the ground into a quagmire of liquid mud. This precluded the use of any vehicles, and our tanks could not support closely the battalion in either attack or defence and were nearly useless. The Germans, on the other hand with their broader tracks could operate and in any case they had a lateral road for movement. No anti-tank guns could be moved up to resist the counter attack.
>
> The putting out of action of the wireless set at the critical moment in Hoven, and the cutting of the telephone line.
>
> The failure to secure the start line, though under the circumstances the DCLI would not wish to blame 7 Somerset Light Infantry. They did all they could, tired and depleted as they were.

After we had been relieved by the Wiltshire's, I saw Brigadier Essame in his headquarters. He was subdued, but praised the battalion's fighting spirit.

The knowledge that we had suffered some 200 casualties although inflicting many more on the enemy, and the fact that we had been unable to hold on to Hoven weighed heavily on me. But I realised that to have remained would have been committing us to a death trap, situated as it was directly under the shadow of the guns on the Siegfried Line high ground, and nearly two miles ahead of the Americans.

Twice my advise had been rejected. Firstly, when I had warned of the dangers of the attack; secondly, when I urged that we withdraw from our beleaguered position. I was suffering from a sense of shock. General Horrocks, his own face ashen, must have realised this when I met him as I left Brigade Headquarters. "Don't blame yourself, George," he reassured me. "Blame me." Such was the magnanimity of this fine commander. Undoubtedly, he felt he should have over ruled Essame.

Next day, he visited us in our rest area of Kling, and addressed the battalion in the refectory of a monastery there. It was a fine, straightforward speech, and the morale of all ranks burned more brightly because of it.

My depression was to last for some days, and when I heard that I had been awarded a second DSO for operations in September, my first reaction was to refuse the honour. But Lieut Col Aubrey Coade, of the Wiltshire's, calmed me down and made me see sense.

Soon, the day-to-day demands of command allowed me to dwell no longer on the shortcomings of the battle and helped the more robust part of my mind to assert itself. But for many years afterwards, I pondered on the fact that I should have found a better solution for dealing with the enemy who I suspected might come forward to the Gap edge. I should have given my support company commander the role of arranging close covering fire and ensured that the Somerset's were beefed up with extra men and weapons. It is always better in battle to over insure in firepower than to depend on a lesser measure.

So for us of 5DCLI our only defeat in the whole campaign, except for Hill 112 but they said a glorious one. It was wrote, a press officer of Montgomery's 2nd Army staff, "one of the great stories of British participation in the war."

An exaggeration, I thought, but words of comfort and the morale of the battalion remained high. What marvellous soldiers our men can be!"

Not braver than the men of other leading nations but only that our courage lasts longer, wrote Field Marshal Sir William Slim. No doubt based on the history of the 1st World War; being the only Army who fought right through to final Victory from 1914 to 1918 without giving up or having a serious mutiny.

CHAPTER NINE

Winter Woods and Christmas Bells

The soft, cloying mud of that 1944 autumn had put a brake on the Allied sweep towards the Rhine. In fact, the brigade's advance of 4,500 yards was a record on the British northern half of the west front in that cold and rainy autumn of 1944. Now, we would have to wait for the winter frosts to firm up the ground for our armour, and for the longer daylight hours of January. It was a time to consolidate the line, a two-month lull in which to rebuild the battalion and bring it back to its peak of efficiency.

We took our turn at holding the line in Dorset Wood, or in the battalion reserve area of Gillrath. And we took full advantage of these sessions to keep ourselves in fettle for what we hoped would be the final onslaught. It was said in Division that you could always tell where the DCLI were by the sounds of small arms, grenades and mortar fire! (Training). Although we saw little of the enemy, there was no let-up in the business of war throughout December and January. The finer arts of the Vickers machine gun and Crocodile tank flame thrower were demonstrated, subalterns and sergeants discussed platoon tactics; officers gave lectures on the use of other arms, like artillery, vickers machine guns and tanks.

The men kept themselves in trim with PT and brisk bayonet fighting, and Major Hutchins our new B Coy commander obtained good results with his introduction of a new method of close-quarter fighting . . . split second or shot-gun shooting. Our aim was to produce efficient platoons, for these are the bricks with which a good battalion is built. Exercises were held using live ammunition . . . just to ensure that concentration was not allowed to wander.

Sniper suits for the riflemen and leather jerkins for the men of HQ and support companies kept the cold at bay. And there was no shortage of sweaters, scarves, gloves and warm woollen underwear. Which was just as well, for the murky

December days grew steadily colder until, by January, the temperature had plummeted to well below zero.

But the weather in between the snow storms was delightfully crisp and dry and greatly added to our zest for life. In spite of the relentless training, or maybe because of it, the battalion had never been happier in the whole campaign. We did our share of line holding facing an enemy only a few hundred yards away.

Brief respites from training or time out of the line were times to be treasured. The usual routine was four days in contact with the enemy then four days in a reserve position, followed by four days in a rest and training area. We trained in both these latter periods. To wallow in a pit head bath at the mining community of Brunson was luxury indeed!

Then there were the merry parties at the home of Dr Hertenfelt, only five miles from the front line; leave parties at Brussels were in full swing, and soon, we were told, they would be extended to Britain. We held weekly dances, to which the Dutch population flocked. It was the first time they had danced since 1940 and the expressions on those girls faces when doing the "Boomps-a-daisy" was a sight to behold. It was a time for rejoicing. The Dutch kindness and hospitality was very great and the conduct of our men won golden opinions. "I have never seen troops as good as yours" said one Burger-master who had lived through two wars. The British army system of leadership and discipline should take the credit mainly for this excellent behaviour.

Field Marshal Montgomery decorating Captain David Willcocks with the ribbon of the Military Cross.

One day, in the pouring rain and against a background noise of small arms and mortar fire, the divisional commander presented 5DCLI with decorations resulting from the operations around Arnhem. These comprised a DSO for me an MC (Major Fry), two DCM's, and five MM's adding to the DSO, three MC's and one MM that Monty had bestowed upon us a week earlier for the Normandy fighting. General Thomas carried out the ceremony in a boxing ring. He had the reputation of being a hard man, but I noticed there were tears in his eyes as he pinned to my DSO the bar from his Military Cross that he had so gallantly won in the First World War.

The battalion was getting back to fighting strength. Major Hutchins, holder of the Military Cross, had joined us from 50 Division. Others were Major Roberts and Captain Jobson, who had been wounded early in the Normandy campaign. Captain Sayers took over the anti-tank platoon, and with Sgt Richards soon re-built it into an efficient fighting unit following the severe losses of inflicted on it in the grim ordeal of Hill 112. Of all my sub units it had been the slowest to recover.

Our role in the wood was a low profile one, patrolling only a night to conceal the fact that 43 Div had relieved 52 Lowland, who were shortly to launch an offensive to bring us abreast of the river Roer, which was the only obstacle before the Cologne plain. The Americans would attack on the right, with 43 Div coming in later to provide the finishing touches. The operation was to be known as "Blackcock".

While I was at last able to fit in my postponed Christmas leave, my excellent and most loyal number two, Major Andy Martin, took over 5DCLI for a few days. The battalions chief difficulty in planning patrols was to find a safe way out of the wood.

It had been occupied by many units, and each had laid mines profusely and had not always recorded them accurately. The Germans, too, had left behind their share, especially the wooden "Schumine".

But the Germans were not our only enemy in that winter of 1945. Despite ample supplies of thick clothing, snow suits and rubber boots, special efforts had to be made to keep the men warm. The rear ares were scoured for stoves, which, with the aid of "fireplaces" improvised from biscuit tins, provided some comfort even if they did change ruddy complexions to sooty black ones!

But this did not matter, as a scheme was worked out whereby 100 men a day were sent to Brunsun for baths. The added bonus was that besides the sheer bliss of wallowing in hot water, it meant four hours out of the line. The forward companies were changed over every two days. Feet were washed and fresh socks put on daily. After 14 days of the most severe weather, we had only four cases of frostbite or Trench foot. Towards the end of our stay in Dorset Wood, we were privileged to have a grandstand view, of the capture of Straten and Hetteralh, as the 52nd Division steadily bit their way into enemy positions.

Soon, in the forward companies area, we were able to stand upright, untroubled by sniper or mortar fire. In the second part of the month came details for the final stage of Operation Blackcock. We were to be given the opportunity of recapturing Hoven, where we had suffered our only defeat in the chill of the November rain.

Greatly refreshed from my leave, I went with Captain Anslow to Brigade HQ, where we stayed for several days planning the operation with Brigadier Essame. The operation order consisted of 14 pages. The battalion was taken out of the line a few days beforehand to plan for the attack, in which Crocodile flamethrowers were to be used. Then, on January 24, word came that the Germans were falling back, and 1 Worcestershire, my old battalion, breached the minefields to cheat us out of the satisfaction of settling our score. They moved in without opposition, derisively pinning our operation order to a farmhouse door.

Moving in two columns of the New Kangaroo personnel carriers, we pushed out east and west of the notorious Hoven Wood next day to occupy Kraudorf, and then moved several miles north after the retreating Germans to Nuin and Ronderalt.

I had leapt at the chance when Brigadier Essame had

offered us the use of these gargantuan vehicles which the Canadians had first used so successfully in Normandy. They were tanks with the lids removed and each could carry 10 men with many advantages, or converted SP guns. They could keep up with the tanks and, in an assault, could carry the infantry on to, or near, their objective; they were proof against artillery and mortar fire, except from a direct hit, and could keep small fire arms fire out.

The drivers, from the RASC or a Canadian unit, were both brave and skilled. For some reason, my fellow COs in the brigade were lukewarm on the idea of the Kangaroos, so we got them.

Our task accomplished, we were immediately relieved and moved back into Holland, where, after a day's journey, we arrived at Kamp, near Nuth, a pleasant and rolling country unfouled by the hand of war. After a stay in Grotenrath, on the German side of the Dutch border, we were moved, in the middle of December, deeper into Holland to the village of Barr, completely unspoilt by the war. It was the first stage of the Division's movement to a concentration area at Tillburg, in Belgium, in preparation for operations in the Reichwald area in January.

But first, the battalion was looking forward to two weeks of Christmas festivities out of the line. The long journey started on December 19, in an almost holiday atmosphere. While on the march, the men were confronted by long columns moving in the opposite direction. Urgent messages were passed and an air of excitement was apparent. Something big was afoot.

The end of the day found the DCLI across the Belgian border at Bilsen, near Maastricht. It was there that we heard the startling news that the Germans had struck in great strength against the thinly held American sector in the Ardennes and were heading in full cry for the Meuse.

With a party of other COs and Brigadiers who had been on active service since June and were in need of rest and change, I had just reached Brussels, on my way home for Christmas leave.

We were stopped as we were about to board the plane

home and went to HQ 21 Army Group and told to rejoin our units. But the atmosphere at the Head quarters was one of calm and confidence, and there was an inspiring talk about the speed with which Patton had moved his troops against the southern shoulder of the salient.

The people of Bilsen were apprehensive that the Germans might return, but spared no efforts to provide us with simple comforts and to make the festive atmosphere as homely as possible. We did our best to restore their confidence and although at an hour's notice to move, we were hopeful of spending a happy Christmas there. The immediate task of 30 Corps, which consisted of four war hardened crack divisions . . . the Guards Armoured, 43 Wessex, 51 Highland and 53 Welsh . . . was to block the approach to Brussels. General Horrocks, our corps commander, was reported to have said "let them come . . . we'll 'Waterloo' them!" There is little doubt they would have been a tough proposition for any Germans who dared try cross the Meuse!

Early one morning, a US battalion arrived at the station after a cold, cheerless journey from England. Our cooks turned out to send them on their way with a warming British cuppa. Tales of the American soldier overseas were legendary among our fighting men. Although this group had been in England only a short time before being sent to the front, a wag was heard to shout as they moved off through the village: "How's my wife?"

On Christmas Eve, Lieut Stock, MC, returned from Rheims with another prize; not a stout German sergeant this time, but several cases of champagne and other choice French wines. I had sent him on a wine forage to the famous Champagne district so that the battalion could celebrate Christmas in style. It raised a few French eyebrows to see a British officer calmly sampling the local vintage while the fate of all France was hanging in the balance in the Ardennes.

Christmas day, 1944, in an Order of the day, I paid my own tribute to what I called "one of the greatest fighting battalions of the British Army". And to emphasise the point came news of the award of a DSO for Major Lonsdale, an MC for "Holly" Holland, and MM's for Sgt Yeomans and Cpl Adams . . . the brave little man whose main concern had been in what colour he should sketch the enemy positions during the hell of Hoven.

It was to be the final Christmas of the war and sadly for some their last ever. Sergeants and officers met in a little café to solemnly toast each other with glasses of ale. Each platoon served its own Christmas dinner, and everyone worked hard to achieve a festive atmosphere. We sat down to a feast of tinned turkey, pork, roast potatoes, plum puddings, and apples and oranges . . . with crockery and linen provided by the Belgians.

As CO, I drank the health of each platoon in the customary manner . . . albeit briefly, as David Willcocks and I had to make an afternoons recce of Liege with a view to a counter- attack. The approach road to Liege was alive with US Army trucks being driven with great urgency, and the city streets echoed to the rumble of American traffic moving supplies to the men who were battling to stem the German tide. There was little sign of the festive spirit among the long-suffering populace, who obviously feared the worst.

But for the men of 5DCLI the only encounter was a football match against the 7 Somerset's, which the Cornwall's won 3-2. Cocktail parties were in full swing for the officers, while the sun showed off the frosty winter landscape to its best Christmas card effect. It was during an evening party at Brigade headquarters that news came that we were to move forward to meet a possible fresh enemy thrust. The festivities broke up promptly. Bill Gorman the Adjutant relates amusingly that after the Christmas parties before going to bed he took what he thought was Aspirin but it was Benzerdine, which kept him awake most of the night checking and rechecking the battalions march tables for the mechanised march the next day and making sure that the companies fully understood all details.

At 5 O'clock on a bitterly cold morning, while the town slept, our long column of motor transport moved off. Our destination was the village of Elsloo and Catsop.

High Command had anticipated every possible plan that the Germans could conceive, like:

* Airborne landings behind the US Army Sector in confunction with a thrust on Aachen.
* Strong thrusts with armour or infantry through Rotgen or Eupen, or both.
* Diversionary attacks on US or British sectors.

To counter these, we prepared to:

* Move at an hour's notice for action against airborne attacks.
* Occupy the area of Houtendove Kling, near Brunson, and dig in as a divisional lay-back.
* Occupy the area in the US sector below Aachen.
* Counter attack through, or round, firm bases occupied by 129 or 130 Bdes with the object of sealing off any enemy penetration.

The battalion was involved in a little bit of aerial drama on New Years Day, while General Rawlings, the active divisional commander, was inspecting our position. He was deputizing for General Thomas, who was temporarily commanding 30 Corps in the Ardennes. General Rawlings, conspicuous in his red cap band and trimmings, was walking over the forward slopes when several German fighters swooped in barely 50 ft above his head.

They were the survivors of a squadron that had successfully attacked the Allied aerodromes, leaving many of our planes blazing and smoking on the ground. But they had stayed too long on the job and paid a high price in pilots for their dashing attack. One of them fell victim to groundfire from Sgt Sampson's platoon . . . a timely demonstration of the battalion's striking power for the General! Sampson a great fighter and the holder of the MM had been wounded in Normandy, and on his way back to us had passed through a reinforcement Depot, there with others they had been lectured to by a Doctor who said that they had been wounded by being careless. Sampson complained to me and I understood that the Chief of Staff, General de Guingand said that this confirmed other reports and the eccentric doctor was moved.

Otherwise, the year got off to a relatively peaceful start, and our routine of work, training and happy social evenings continued until January 11, when we were promptly ordered to move to Dorset wood. It was the coldest day recorded in many years in that border country between Holland and Germany, and we had great difficulty in getting the frozen tracks of the carriers moving.

CHAPTER TEN

Operation Veritable

The battle of Bulge was over. Hitler's desperate last-grasp attempt to seize the initiative with a massive push by thirteen infantry and five panzer divisions along an 80 mile front of lightly held US Positions in the Ardennes in eastern Belgium, had been effective but short lived.

For a time it had been touch and go. Taken completely by surprise the American casualty toll had been high. But they had rallied and shown great courage and initiative under adverse conditions. History proves it to be one of their great victories. By the end of the battle they had suffered some 80,000 casualties, as opposed to the 100,000 of the Germans in the coldest winter of the war. It was more than the battered Third Reich could bear.

The enemy had chosen to fight in front of the obstacle of the Rhine, and now he was to take the consequences of this strategical decision. Under the operational code name "Veritable", the allies were to destroy them between the rivers Maas and Rhine. We of 43 Div were to revert to 30 Corps, now released from the Ardennes fighting, which, in turn, would become attached to the Canadian Army. Other British divisions were soon to follow suit, which meant that the British units were fighting under Canadian command. 30 British Corps (General Sir Brian Horrocks) was for this battle under the command of the 1st Canadian Army, whose Commander was General Crerar a strong independent minded Canadian whose relationship with Field Marshal Montgomery was not as good as it should have been. However Horrocks had a high opinion of him.

The 1st Canadian Army consisting of both Canadian and British Divisions had captured the strongly fortified Channel Port and opened the way for the capture of the great port of Antwerp thus protecting the left flank of the advance of the 2nd British Army. The Canadians with their British

Divisions had done a magnificent job though at a heavy cost in fierce fighting.

Meanwhile, the British 2nd Army would hold the Maas with only a skeleton force. Their main task was to plan the Rhine crossing to follow the effects of "Veritable" with great speed.

The operation meant the movement of some 200,000 troops, with their tanks, 3,500 vehicles, guns and ammunition, mostly from the far south to the assembly area near Nijmegen. This miracle was achieved over roads both frozen and flooded by rapid thaws, completely undetected by the Germans. We of 5DCLI moved north, and after a long journey reached Vassetaer, between Tillburg and Antwerp. The thunder of our anti-aircraft barrage reverberated amid the spluttering drone of the enemy's doodlebugs as the Germans incessantly tried to slow down the flow of supplies through the deep-water Belgian port.

For four days in early February, we were fully briefed on the plan at a place called St Oedenrobe, near Nijmegen. An operations room was organised and stocked with maps and air photos. Training in street fighting and the crossing of obstacles was carried out.

After seven months of front line battle experience, the battalion had reached its zenith in efficiency. Its leaders were experienced, and not found wanting; the men of the rifle companies were well trained and hardened; and the specialists and administrative personnel were experts in their fields.

In late afternoon of February 9th, we were part of the long Brigade column that began to wind its way forward to Nijmegen. Towards late evening we arrived in the salient; all was quiet and little could be seen except for the occasional star shell or very light probing in the night's dark shadows.

It was difficult to realise that how, packed in those silent woods and houses that surrounded us, was the greatest concentration of men, artillery and tanks since Normandy bridgehead days. Crerar was an expert gunner and thoroughly believed in concentrating his artillery to overwhelm the enemy.

At 5 am, the calm of the early morning had been shattered by the combined roar of 1,200 artillery pieces, and the fire had continued for five hours and the fire plan included in its final stage a 'Pepperpot' the fire of medium machine guns, Bofors and tank guns to keep the enemy's heads down. The three British divisions and one Canadian had gone in . . . the enemy, numbed by half a million rounds of high explosive, had been able to offer only a patchy resistance.

We were put at one hour's notice to move on February 10th, our task being to follow up 15 Scottish Div and exploit their success in the direction of Goch, in fact to capture the town. We moved towards our start position at 9 pm that night in our vehicles and tanks, watching the Kaleidoscope of colour as the coloured tracer of our artillery cut its beautiful patterns across the night sky in pursuit of German attack aircraft.

With two divisions using the Nijmegen-Cleve road and with the enemy putting up fierce resistance at the head of the column, our progress was slow.

The long night was bitterly cold, with flurries of icy rain and driving sleet. There were few hand-holds on the cold steel surface of the tanks on which the men travelled and no room to lie down. There were frequent stops but no official halts as the column wound its apprehensive way forward. No one knew if these stops would last five minutes or five hours, so it was only possible now and then to jump down and stamp life back into frozen feet. General Horrocks afterwards acknowledged that he had made a mistake in releasing his first reserve too soon. The 15 Scottish had given him a misleading report of their progress and one of their Brigades had not even taken part in the battle.

The men's fighting spirit was at its lowest ebb when the first glimmer of dawn penetrated that seemingly endless night. But now came another problem . . . feeding a battalion spread out over three miles along a crowded road.

The nights turmoil had brought its embarrassment for some. A Brigade of 43rd Div had been ordered to by-pass the town of Cleive, but had taken a wrong turning in the tangle of roads lying to the south of the town.

They ended up driving straight into the town centre, much to the surprise of the German garrison and the fury of the Scots 15 Div, who were preparing a dawn attack, the resulting street fighting was fast and furious. Even the officers and men of Brigade HQ found themselves in close-quarter battles. Finally the good news filtered back to us: Cleive had been taken! Now, we were told, 5DCLI would by-pass the Reichwald Forest by moving along the axis of the Materhorn Goch road and capture Goch, some 10 miles away, a tall order, we felt, as only a very small area of the Reichwald had been cleared of Germans.

Air photos of the town and its approaches were studied, and plans made for dealing with the hidden menaces of the forest on the way. A strong fire base consisting of 3 in mortars and machine guns would be established among the hummocks just west of the Forest, which, with artillery, would protect our right flank.

The first round from a German gun would be the signal for the wood to be covered with fire and smoke. Impatiently, in the early afternoon, we waited along the track which winds its way up to the north east corner of the Reichwald for information regarding the enemy's positions. But when we heard that the recce unit concerned were engaged in hostilities in the hamlet of Sealhof and held up, we decided to deal with the situation ourselves. The unit was pulled back while our artillery and mortars softened up the opposition, and then Major Lonsdale's D coy, supported by tanks, swept in to finish the job in house-to-house battles in the fading light. The Germans fell back into Materhorn. Before pursuing them, I formulated a plan whereby we could keep one company on the move by by-passing the village between the road and the edge of the forest. This decision had been prompted by the fact that while B Coy and its tanks and the regrouping of armoured vehicles of the recce unit had been assembling on the open road, not a shot had been fired at us from those sinister looking woods. We were a wonderful target.

I came to the conclusion that at this stage of the battle there were no enemy troops facing 53 Welsh Div, and if patrols had been sent forward they would have found this to be correct. The great lesson is never lose touch with the enemy. Ground could only have been won easily. It was some hours later that General von Luttwitz moved his XLVII Panzer Corps into the Reichwald, and they met the Welshmen head-on. A violent battle ensued before they were defeated and the forest cleared of Germans. But the cost to the 53rd was very high.

There was just time to brief the company in the fast fading light. They were to take the road near the corner of the forest, just south of Hau. The ground was too soft for vehicles or tanks to accompany them. Meanwhile we hoped to catch the enemy off balance by smashing through Materhorn with the tanks and, using the road, press on to link up with B Coy. But despite the German's night defeat in Sealhof, they were better organised than we thought, and were reinforced with tanks and support guns.

The Materhorn attack seemed doomed from the start. First, one of the tanks carrying the three C Coy platoons refused to start; then, just when the advance was nicely under way on the road leading to the village, the Germans opened up with their 88's. The men crouched on the cold, inhospitable armour plating of the tanks tried to make themselves as small as mice as the tracer and shrapnel flashed and crashed around them. The first tank, carrying Lieut Bruce Jones and his men of 15 Platoon, burst into flames after taking two bazookas' hits. And to add to our misery the heavy rain that had begun soon after that attack started, turned into snow.

While C Coy were engaged in their firm encounter north of Materhorn, I had sent D Coy round to the right to attack from the south west. They fared no better. After crossing a series of water-filled ditches in the dark and fighting for hours, the men were soaked to the skin and nearly dropping from fatigue, mostly the effect of the previous night. Discretion, I decided, must be the better part of valour. I called the whole thing off. The battalion had to be rested and fed and then, we could make a better job of it on the morrow.

By then, it was 3 am. B Coy had arrived back, bringing nine prisoners. They had reached their destination but their communications had failed and they had lost touch with Battalion HQ and I was very anxious about their fate. Fortunately, Major Hutchins, after waiting for some time and seeing no sign of a battalion breakthrough, had wisely decided to come back. Without tanks or anti-tank guns, the company would have been in an extremely vulnerable position.

But B Coy's mission had not been in vain. Undoubtedly, this force, moving about in the dark and taking prisoners, must have an alarming effect on the enemy and weakened their grip on the Materhorn area and that part of the Reichwald.

The battalion regrouped quickly in Saalhof, bolstered by a few hours sleep and some food, Very much refreshed, we discussed the situation with the brigadier, who had come forward in the early morning to see us.

We decided that 'H' hour for our final assault would be at 1400 hours. When we had captured Materhorn, 7 Somerset Light Infantry would push through towards Goch. But it was by now obvious that the enemy had anticipated our intentions in the Reichwald, and they had greatly strengthened their front there by moving up troops from the American Roer area aided by the flooded river, were to contain the Americans for nearly three weeks till the flood subsided.

Our attack went like clockwork. Covered by artillery fire and supported by the tanks of 4/7 Dragoon Guards, we went forward in style. With C Coy keeping the Germans busy on the left, A Coy penetrated on the right, and quickly took half the village. B and D Companies then leap-frogged through to complete the task.

Such was the precision of the attack, that the enemy were unable to put up much of a fight. We swept through, taking prisoners and a considerable amount of equipment. Our own casualties were light. With the village firmly in our hands, the Somerset's poured through I met their CO Lieut Col Reeves, a very fine soldier, on the easter exit and discussed the situation.

The capture of Materhorn facilitated the advance of the 3rd Canadian Division who were fighting on our left in the flooded polder – they called themselves 'Water-rats'. Instead of tanks they used water borne armoured buffaloes.

The Germans were putting up a dogged fight in open country beyond the village in the Materhorn-Hau area, but their main line was in wired and entrenched positions beyond Hau corner.

Meanwhile, the Welsh Division, which included regular English and Scots battalions, were pushing steadily forward in the Reichwald area, despite bitter opposition from the enemy paratroops. Such is the speed of war that Materhorn soon became a back area, and our artillery moved in to become our unwelcome near-neighbours. Even being at the right end of the big guns, with their constant bark and blast, was no comfort to us and certainly did little for our already stretched nerves.

Our short stay in the village experienced us in another aspect of war . . . the German refugee problem. This we solved by concentrating them in the church.

Feeding them was no problem, as the German houses were well stocked with supplies, and we all dined in style.

But the sound of battle raged constantly in our ears. The Germans were defending stubbornly their main position beyond Hau, and were counter attacking with tanks of 116 Panzer Division, which had been ordered to retake Cleve.

The Panzer Division fiercely resisted by the British Infantry, were at the same time taking a severe mauling from the massed fire of the Corps artillery. By the evening of February 13, 4 Wiltshire's, of 129 Bde, were able to get a footing on the high ground Square Wood east of the Cleve Forest. But important as this and advances by other divisions were, they did nothing to diminish the ferocity of the fighting. Now was to follow the most bitter period of the whole operation.

The German Army had now plainly elected to fight west of the Rhine and it was here that it had to be defeated. No longer was the success of our division to be assessed in the ground gained, but in the number of German dead that strewed the shell-ravaged farmland and in the demoralised prisoners who passed in a steady stream into the corps' cage, but the 40,000 enemy Paratroops and the men of the 116 Panzer Division and 15 Panzer Grenadier Division were fighting well.

The advance of 214 Bde to Hau and 129 Bde to Bedburg had eased the situation at Cleve, but the enemy had dropped back to a new defensive position barring the way to Calcar and Goch.

The German line ran from the woods around Moyland, across a low feature known as the Eselberg, a mile south of Bedburg, to Cleve forest. The allies advance route to the south was completely blocked.

Major General Thomas caught a chill and was confined to his operations caravan. But despite a high temperature and the roar of surrounding guns day and night, giving him little chance to rest, he persisted in directing operations, aided by the brigade commander, Brigadier Essame. The brigadier would relate how, after being out all day going round the division and co-ordinating operations, he would arrive tired and often wet at the general's caravan as dusk was falling. There would be the divisional commander, ensconced in bed and wrapped in a brightly coloured dressing gown.

Said Brigadier Essame: "After my report, we would discuss matters and then he would give his directions to me in an atmosphere of Eno Salts and aspirins.

The tenacity of the German defenders was typified by the gallant and, for a time, successful resistance shown by a company of paratroopers in Square Wood.

The wood was raked and reraked by our artillery fire, and then by the terrible blasts of our rocket projectors and RAF Typhoons, until at last the few shocked survivors could do no more. In lay-back positions in Materhorn, it was becoming obvious that our services would again soon be required, so we spent our time training and studying a sand model of the country around and beyond Square Wood.

To a large extent, we were having to live off the land, for

the supply roads from Beek to Kranonburg were under water, having been flooded by the retreating Germans. Supplies were brought up by Dukws, with ammunition as a priority. The expected summons came on the night of February 15. The brigade was to go into action next day, to capture the high ground to the north east of Goch. This was a small plateau with a gentle rise which ended in an escarpment just north east of the River Niers. It was to be a four-battalion attack; 1 Worcester would go in on the right and 7 Somerset on the left, with limited objectives. The 5DCLI and 4 Somerset's would exploit the south to get on to the high ground overlooking Goch.

FEB 1945

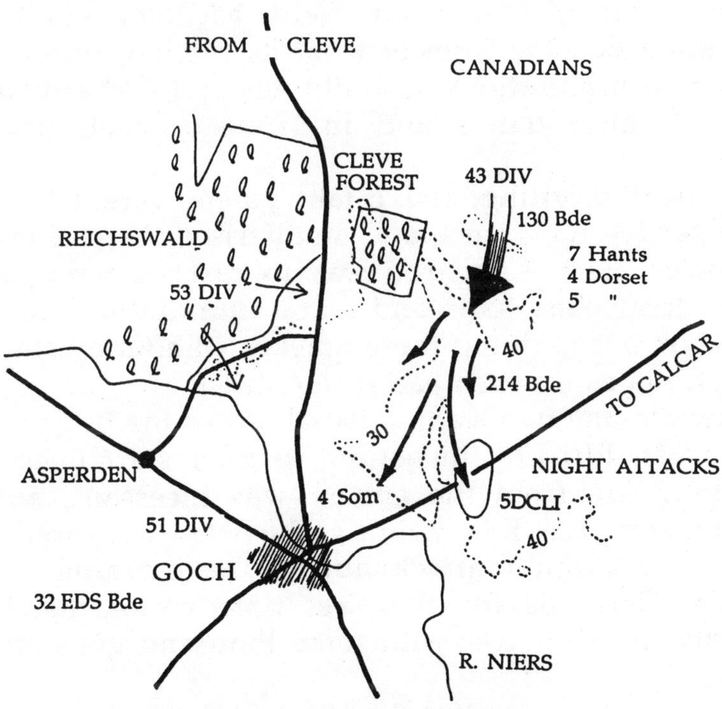

THE ADVANCE BY 43 DIV TO GOCH

15, 16, & 17 FEB. 1945

CONTOURS IN METRES

Scale – 1:100,000

0 1 2 3 4

MILES

Our attack was to start in fading light, with the Somerset's following at 0100 hours, in the early hours of the morning. We were to advance in five armoured columns of tanks and Kangaroo armoured troop carriers, with a carrier and Jeep column coming up behind, 100 armoured vehicles moving in a solid phalanx, as practised by German armour in the desert.

D Coys objective was a small settlement called Schresshof, while B Coy would take the hamlet of Bergmanshof. Once these had fallen, C Coy would pass through to seize a small rise in the ground that we called Kidney Ridge, because of it's shape.

A Coy held in battalion reserve, would take a large farmhouse in which the battalion command post was to be located. The artillery fire plan, worked out with Lieut Col Wildbore Smith, DSO, our field artillery regimental commander, took the form of what he termed 'prophylactic fire', short concentrations on buildings and orchards on the outer and inner flanks and in front of each company column.

Early next morning, the infantrymen were allotted to their respective Kangaroos and familiarised themselves with the vehicles. Each Kangaroo was to carry compo rations, bundled greatcoats, tools and extra ammunition, and drill was worked out to dump these quickly without crushing the stores as soon as the men had dismounted.

Meanwhile, the two leading battalions of the brigade were having great difficulty in getting to their start lines. Shell and mortar fire from the enemy was incessant, and the battalion from 129 Bde holding the start line area came under heavy counter attack during the morning. In this battle the Germans for the first time could match our superiority in fire power with some thousand guns and 700 mortars.

H-Hour, starting time for the attack, was put back from 11 am to 3 pm.

As soon as word came through, we of 5DCLI prepared to move to our assembly area near Bedburg. There was just time for a quick brew up before the unwieldy tanks and

Kangaroos swung out on to the road. Just when we seemed to be making steady progress, the long iron column ground to a halt. What the hell was going on up there? The minutes were ticking away and if we did not reach our forming-up area before dark the whole thing would end in failure.

I went forward and found the way blocked by anti-tank guns and carriers of the two assault battalions. Tempers all round were on a short fuse. We pushed the offending vehicles off the road, and we went on forward, reaching our start line just before dark . . . now we were on our way . . . it was dark and from the left came the fire of those deadly German 88 guns. Shells were whistling over our heads. I had a horrible vision of some of our armoured vehicles being hit and acting as a beacon for accurate mortar fire. I therefore said to Kitch (Major Kitchen) take your company and escorting tanks to the right and see if you can find a route further away from the Germans on our left. Meanwhile I halted our column. Though there was some mortar fire crashing down not far away they fortunately did not get on to us. Then came the message on the radio, good route a line of pylons moving forward slowly. I therefore swung the whole of the column to the right and caught up B Company. Following the line of Pylons – steel sentinels like something out of a science fiction story. In about an hour and a half we were on the objective. The riflemen decanted quickly and supported by the tanks quickly over ran the enemy who included two 88 mm guns and their crews. We had surprised the enemy and easily rounded up a considerable number of prisoners and capturing transport moving on the Calcar – Goch road.

Through the deafening roar of the Kangaroo engines, messages were being passed to me in the command vehicle. Then came the code words for which I had been waiting. The forward companies had achieved their objectives.

Now for Kidney Ridge, as C Coy went forward, it was obvious from the hurried, haphazard artillery fire that the enemy had little idea of what was happening.

In the half-light of a misty dawn, Kitch, while visiting his platoons, had a brush with an enemy patrol, and dispensed with most of them with his sten.

The night was ours. More than 50 of the enemy had been killed, 100 prisoners taken, and our booty included two 88 guns, a pom-pom and an assorted collection of vehicles.

The deadly 88 Gun captured by the Batallion in the Reichwald battle

Our own losses totalled three. Sadly, they included our provost sergeant Sgt Barret, a mighty puncher in the battalion boxing ring, who had been killed by a shell. The morning mist was a blessing, as it enabled companies to distribute their rations, water and ammunitions to the platoons safe from the prying eyes of the enemy. It finally cleared to reveal a dull flat landscape with scattered farms and small orchards. The Germans did not take long to pin-point our whereabouts, and then things began to get hot. For three days we came under shell and mortar fire, with D and B Companies really having a bad time.

Major Hutchins, D Company commander, was wounded by a splinter, and Lieut Beaver and his men worked gallantly under fire to free trapped comrades when shells fell on D

Coy trenches. A salve of shells fell on the farm buildings that made up battalion HQ. Ironically, the only casualties were some German refugees who had been sheltering in a barn. The signallers under splendid leadership, worked incessantly to repair communication lines that were constantly being broken by the heavy fire, but in the end we had to depend entirely on wireless. A troop commander of the 4/7th Dragoons estimated that 1,000 bombs and shells had hit one orchard in 12 hours!

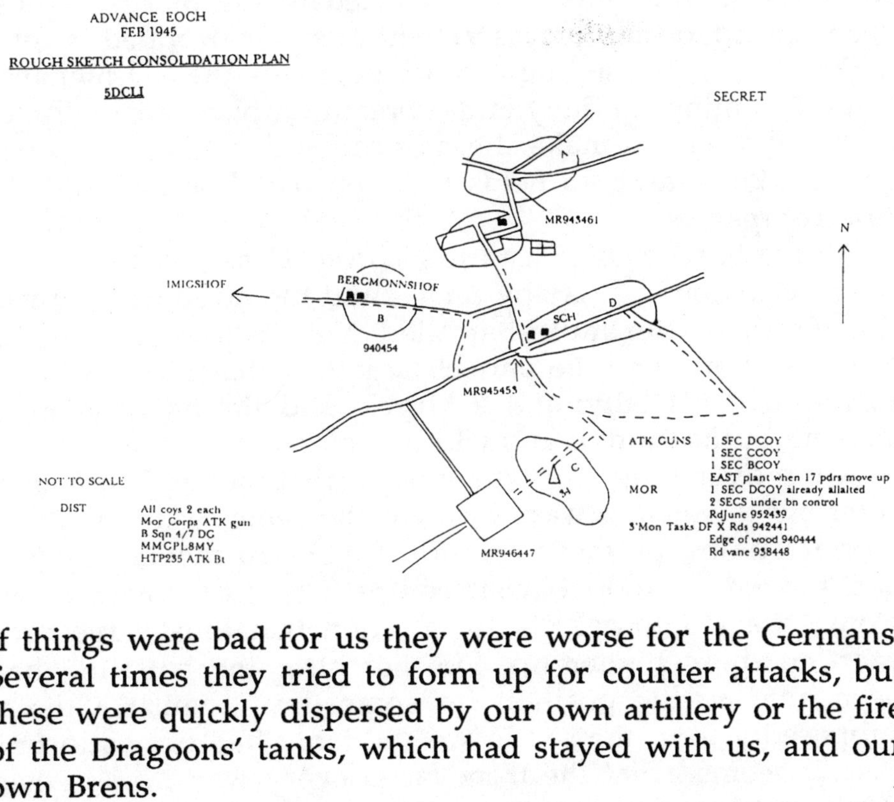

If things were bad for us they were worse for the Germans. Several times they tried to form up for counter attacks, but these were quickly dispersed by our own artillery or the fire of the Dragoons' tanks, which had stayed with us, and our own Brens.

All these attempts were mounted in daylight, for, curiously, the German tactical doctrine did not believe in night attacks . . . the one way they might have countered the superior firepower of our artillery. Good soldiers that they were, there was, perhaps, some defect in the German character which did not allow him to steel his nerves and keep going forward in the dark, unlike his British counterpart. The 7 Somerset's pushed through us and occupied the escarpment, along which a belt of trees ran on our right. This still left us to hold the sensitive flank.

Within our holding area was a building which the German civilians called *Spiershof*; but to us it was simply *Halfway House*, and a more appropriate name could not have been chosen!

For a week it formed the HQ of our anti-tank platoon, during which time they were hosts to the Mortar Platoon, and others from the Gunners, Somerset's and Wiltshire's. All sorts of itinerants were attracted to the place . . . lost despatch riders, and an assortment of strays dropped in for a night or two. It was the contact point for the maintenance column coming up daily and a breathing place generally for those who had to make the hazardous dash over the open tracks across the bare fields between battalion HQ and the rifle companies.

All roads seemed to lead to *Halfway House*, and each had their disadvantages. Go by carrier and the noise would incur the wrath of the multi-barrelled Nebelwerfer mortar; on foot, and you were the perfect target for the sniper wanting to improve his tally; and a bicycle had the nasty habit of sticking in the mud at an awkward moment.

All movements, in whatever direction, and however carefully planned, always brought the same result, a hail of mortar bombs, or shells or both. I gave up moving by jeep and moved on foot to visit companies. 'Just where is the front?' we would ask . . . a question that must have been exerting those higher up, too. For after the battalion had been holding the position for some days against a threat supposedly from the south, we suddenly had orders to face east. It seemed that the front faced every way . . . We had stuck our neck out.

On February 19, the Canadians (Essex Scottish), who had fought their way forward and were now echeloned behind us, came under heavy counter attack during the night, and to some extent were overrun. This meant making changes in our layout, and A Coy, under Major Roberts, were told to occupy buildings to the left rear of battalion HQ. As we at battalion HQ came under harassing artillery and even sniper fire.

On moving forward over what was thought to be safe ground, they were suddenly pinned down by heavy artillery fire. They stayed low in ditches until nightfall, when they advanced and occupied the farm buildings without incident. There was no further mysterious shelling or sniper fire, only signs which showed a small party of the enemy had occupied one of the buildings, which was only 300 yards from Battalion HQ.

The following afternoon, 4 Somerset's Light Infantry moved through us to the east to attack Halvanboon, using our tank squadron and some of the Kangaroos. Unfortunately, Spandaus caught one of the companies dismounting from the Kangaroos and mortar and artillery fire inflicted 40 casualties. But the village was taken. The fighting had been bitter, and the Somerset's had lost many men in a hail of shell and mortar fire, including their C Coy commander, Major Mallalieu, who had been in the forefront of the battle since Normandy.

Our tank commander, Major David Richards, of 4/7 Dragoon Guards, had risen to the occasion magnificently, leading both the infantry and tanks until Halvanboon was safe in Allied hands. He certainly earned his DSO.

The Canadians had also won back some lost ground, at Moyland Wood and a stretch of watery wasteland north of Cleve, so we of 5DCLI were spared further contact with the enemy.

For the next two or three days, we remained in the brigade reserve area, forming a lay-back position should the Germans retake them. Goch had fallen on February 21 after stiff fighting by 51 and 15 divisions. In two weeks, 30 Corps had taken 10,000 prisoners.

On the afternoon of February 23, we were suddenly relieved by the Irish Guards, who arrived in a huge convoy of three-tonners, tired, we made our way back to battered Cleve. The performance of 43 Div in this series of battles might have proved to be the turning point of 'Operation Veritable' according to the 30 Corps History. It says:

"In spite of a very fierce series of counter attacks by some of the best enemy troops, it (43 Div) had outflanked and rolled up the German lay-back position, and had opened up the way to Goch from the north." The enemy had fought hard fighting for his homeland, we had to face a lot of enemy artillery fire and the usual quantity of skilfully directed Mortar fire. Though we had a superiority in tanks, mud and the wet conditions limited their use. So the main burden fell on our British and Canadian Infantry, supported by our superb artillery. During those weeks of battle the battalion was at the top of it's form and our casualties were not as high as I had feared . . . some 90 'All Ranks'. Undoubtedly our excellent standard of training helped to reduce losses. The co-operation between all arms Infantry-Armour and artillery was exemplary – we all had great confidence in each other illustrated by the sudden switch of axis in our advance and the quick rearrangement made by the Gunners under Colonel Wildbore Smith of the 'Fire plan' what he termed Prophylactic fire. Today our fine Regimental system hinders close co-operation but by insuring that most Captains in our Army are attached for some months to other Arms this hindrance can be righted.

Later in the day, we contacted the Canadians on our right in the Hochwald. They had had a hard battle, and seemed to find it difficult to believe that we were on their flank already. They were having to regroup before pushing on, which meant us having to cool our heels in Marienbaum for the time being.

Not that this was any hardship; the stoutly built houses afforded snug billets and were a welcome change from the unpleasant conditions of the past few days. Meanwhile, the Engineers were busy replacing blown bridges with Baileys and the Reme were bulldozing the felled trees from the road.

During the night, our patrols discovered that the Germans had fallen back down the road to Xanten fabled birthplace of Wagners Siegfried. The road ran parallel to the river, which was only two miles away, and as overlooked for most of the way by the spire of Xanten church, which the Germans were no doubt using as an observation post.

But nature again dealt us a winning hand. The early morning river mist of a cold March day shrouded our movement, and we sped forward along the unerringly straight road, the anti-tank guns leap-frogging forward with the rifle companies, trails on the ground ready to open fire. We took 17 surprised German prisoners.

We halted a mile from the town and dug in rapidly, tucking away our vehicles behind the few farm buildings available. Our protective measures were not in vain. As the mist began to clear, the enemy sent over a couple of smoke ranging shots, then the shells and mortar bombs began to fall thick and fast. A troop of the Reconnaissance Regt went forward to engage the enemy, but were thwarted by a huge crater 700 yards down the road that was covered by a malevolent Spandau.

We could now see clearly the great Roman arch of Xanten, once a frontier station of the old empire. The Germans started an accurate and fearsome mortar straff, which they kept up all day. Xanten constituted part of the final perimeter of the Germans' final bridgehead across the Rhine, and they were determined to hold it at all costs. Their resolve was strengthened by a deep anti-tank ditch, minefields, and deeply dug gun emplacements. We were later to find that mines had been timed to blow up within the town two weeks after the Germans' departure, but our sappers were to discover the plot in time.

Two battalions of crack troops of 16 Panzer Regt were under direct orders of the Fuhrer to hold the position 'to the last man and the last round'. We watched as a company of Canadians went in with fixed bayonets to clear the area to our right to make a firm base for an attack on the high ground to the east of Xanten. They suffered heavy casualties as they were caught in open ground by intensive artillery and mortar fire. I spoke to some of them as they struggled back, decimated, past the DCLI battalion command post. Their veterans complained that their *zombies*, young conscripts fresh from training, were no match for the battle-hardened veterans of the Reich. But as a whole the Canadians had fought very well indeed as we would expect. It was by now obvious that nothing short of an all-out attack, with special assault equipment, was going to clear this last enemy strong-hold west of the Rhine. The 4 Somerset's and 4 Wiltshire's were selected from 43 Div to press home the final blow with 2 Canadian Div. This time there was no mistake, and the combined Canadian and British force secured all objectives after heavy fighting. The battered and depleted Germans retreated over the river on this sector. We remained for a time in the Cleve area, resting and training. Occasionally, the enemy shelled the town from across the Rhine, something we found particularly irksome. One accepted a bombardment during the heat of battle, but in a rest area, well, it was the equivalent to operating outside trade union hours.

The respite was to be all too brief. We were put on stand-by to relieve the Canadians, who were being pinned into the gap between the Hochwald and the Balberger Wald.

Our 129 Bde, moving forward on the afternoon of February 26 to take over high ground overlooking Calcar, which had been captured by the Canadian 6 Bde, found many burnt out tanks which had become sitting targets for the Germans after becoming bogged down in the soft mud. We of 5DCLI were to take over from the Cameron Highlander's of Ottawa. They had taken the position in a night attack only 12 hours earlier, and the area was littered with German dead as we made our way forward up a single muddy track.

We stayed there for two days, braving shelling and mortar fire and heavy rain. Then we edged our way forward on the right to the eastern edge of the plateau, attracting further considerable attention from the enemy gunners.

Now we could see clearly the Hochwald, two or three miles to the east, the red houses and the greenery shining like a welcoming beacon in the strengthening sunlight, a welcome contrast to the mud and rain of the previous few days.

Then the brigade was on the move again. The 7 Somerset's, who were in the lead, moved patrols into a wood, just beyond a formidable anti-tank ditch, after mopping up a short lived enemy rearguard action just west of Marienbaun.

I met the Somersets' CO, Lieut Col Reeves, and we made arrangements for the Cornwalls to take over. A Coy were brought up to cover sappers building a Bailey Bridge over the ditch to replace a bridge that had been blown up by the Germans.

We also decided to send forward a fighting patrol into Marienbaun to see if it was occupied. The Somerset's had reported the wood and houses lining the road leading into the village clear of Germans.

But we fell victim to a clever German ploy. It turned out that German paratroops had been watching all our movements from their concealed positions in the wood. We learnt later that they had seen Ivor Reeves and myself talking together. As soon as the A Coy platoon got beyond us, on their way to their recce in the village, the enemy opened fire, cut off and unprotected, the platoon desperately called for artillery fire, which was quickly forthcoming. We hoped that, in the fading light, they would be able to fight their way back, but only the rear section finally made it. The loss of the major part of the platoon was a bitter blow to us, but from it remanded us a lesson that was to stand us in good stead for the rest of the campaign: never rely on unsound information and always send forward a daylight fighting patrol in 'leap-frogging' formation . . . with support Brens and mortars always at the ready. The old old lesson of depth.

This wood, then, was to be the battalion's first objective. We attacked under a barrage on a two-company front. The enemy put up little resistance and soon surrendered. We took 15 prisoners and two anti-tank guns. We then deployed on a three-company front, and in this wide formation swept the ground clear and were soon in Marienbaum. Here we took a further 40 prisoners at little cost to ourselves. I judged that rightly, we were only up against a lightly held position in the woods, hence the sweep instead of attacking in depth with one company up as we so often did.

But the way forward was fraught with difficulties. The Germans had neatly obstructed the road by felling the bordering trees with explosives, and had effectively cratered the highway near the red Schloss, a large house on the outskirts of the village.

A mighty Allied army, war hardened and backed by splendid equipment, now lined the west bank of the Rhine, poised for the final assault.

We of 5DCLI had good reason to be proud. We had been in action for 28 days, our only break being 2½ days in Cleve, and our casualties had been comparatively light, some 90.

As we made our way back to Goch, one felt a quiet happiness and thankfulness that the events of the past month, moving through the unfolding drama of the battle, had gone so well. It was now early spring, and we felt it was the harbinger of a summer of peace. Was it a century age, or only yesterday, that we had stirred to the words of Winston Churchill, calling us from the slumber and half-heartedness of the last two decades? It could have been either. Soon, he was to be with us on the Rhine.

We remembered our comrades who had fought and died during the ordeal of our long forward march, Cheux, the first shock of action, and the Panthers, the terrible ordeal of Hill 112, the brilliant storming of Le Plessis, the crossing of the Seine.

The dash and the drama of our breakthrough to Driel to save the remnants of the Airborne at Arnhem, the battle on the railway embankment, fighting shoulder to shoulder with the fearless Americans in the ditches of Orpheusden, the grim battle of Hoven where though defeated the battalion had fought with great determination and inflicted heavy losses on the enemy.

The long weeks holding the line before the Reichwald, the Siegfried Line, the exciting wait in reserve while the

Ardennes battle leaped forward like a great sea and then receded. The advance in the snow and ice to the River Roer in iron monsters, and then this last grim battle of the Reichwald.

One thought with great pride, pleasure and gratitude of the comradeship and selflessness of the men around one; they had given the best that was in them. They knew it and were content. The battle of the Rhineland had been won. It was March 10 and it had been tough going since February 8 the start of the battle. The British had suffered 10,300 casualties and the Canadians 5,250 but had inflicted about 22,000 dead or badly wounded and taken 23,000 prisoners.

CHAPTER ELEVEN

Crossing the Rhine

We were billeted in the small village of Hayan, on the banks of the Maas, which had served as the German front line throughout that bitter winter of 1944/45. It was like a left-over scene from the Great War of a quarter of a century before: the houses stood in ruins, victims of continuous Allied bombardment, the Paschendaele-type trenches cut their way down to the swollen river, surmounted occasionally by the menacing notices 'Minen – verboten!'

Here we stayed for 12 days, enjoying the early spring weather as we honed ourselves and equipment to a new sharpness for Operation Plunder, the crossing of the Rhine and the final thrust into the Nazi heart.

Briefings were carried out meticulously, with fine attention to detail and training was rigourous. There was no way anything was going to go wrong at this late stage. One warm, summery day, during a battalion rifle meet, we gave a brief respite to our targets of bottles and tins to watch the armada of the airborne divisions winding their way through the clear blue sky. Our hearts soared with them.

Soon, it was our turn, but for 5DCLI it meant a cold moonlit march across the long pontoon bridge spanning the mighty river near Rees on the night of March 24/25.

At 3 am, we arrived at Esserden, chilled and desperately in need of sleep. Some of us were lucky enough to get our heads down in a big German farm house, but most were content to huddle in shell scrapes in nearby fields, and to bed down under the stars.

We were alert and ready to go when Brigadier Essame outlined the brigades plan at an orders group in the farmhouse at 9 am. The route forward lay between Diened and Millingen. Two battalions would cross the unfinished autobahn of Megchelin, where it was thought the enemy had established a defensive position and the Cornwalls would pass on in Kangaroos and take the village.

Megchelin was a large settlement on the Dutch side of the border, in flat marshy country. The two leading battalions were to attack early in the afternoon, and we were to hold our positions until 3 pm. A RASC Kangaroo squadron and a troop of Crocodile flame throwers were to join us during the morning, but they had yet to cross the Rhine.

New born lambs skipping in the sunlit meadows made the grim business that lay before us seem somewhat incongruous as we quickly prepared for action.

At the appointed hour, we moved forward and joined up with the Kangaroo squadron with their excellent drivers from the Royal Army Service Corps, who were assembling in a big field alongside the main road.

To our dismay, we found these armoured carriers had, very sensibly, been loaded with 25 pounder shells before crossing the Rhine. Now it was our job to unload them!

After some considerable time spent at this chore, we embarked and the long armoured column was soon on its menacing way to war. Sitting next to the warm, throbbing engine and protected by the steel walls from the rush of cold air, one felt a glow of confidence in these battlehorses that had already carried us forward with little loss on two major operations.

After a steady advance of some miles along these border roads, we came to a sudden standstill. There was fierce fighting ahead, and the Somerset's, through whom we were to advance, were being held up in a dogged action by German paratroopers on the line of the partly constructed autobahn. With Captain Willcocks, I went forward to surmise the situation. There was considerable hostile shelling, and may buildings were on fire. Trees lay shattered and torn by shells and mortar bombs. The vicious staccato of Spandau fire heightened the tension of the situation.

In the middle of all this mayhem we came across a friendly face . . . that of Captain Stock, namesake of the enterprising Max Stock, whose festive forages around the French vineyards had ensured our Christmas being a happy one.

He had been transferred from 5DCLI at about the

beginning of the year and was now a company commander with the Dorset's. They were now engaged in protecting the left rear of 7 Somerset's Light Infantry. Moments later, the gallant Lieut Col Ivor Reeves, of the Somerset's, came down the road, his shoulder shattered. He had been hit while trying to locate the enemy, who, he said, were resisting bitterly. They had even shot down some of their own men who had tried to surrender.

In the fading light, we made our way back to the Kangaroos, which were now under fire. A direct hit on one of the vehicles had disabled a whole section. We decided to wait no longer. Under cover of a smoke-screen, B Coy moved forward in their Kangaroos to attack enemy posts that the Somerset's had reported to be just north of the autobahn. Once this area had been secured, the reserve company would leap-frog through after a short concentration of artillery fire to capture Megchelin. With their escort of tanks, B Coy passed safely through the smoke-enshrouded area which was infested by pockets of German resistance.

In the now fading light, they could just make out the shadowy ridge of the autobahn. Then came a blinding flash. The leading Kangaroo had been hit by a bazooka. The rest of the company quickly disembarked as Spandau and answering Bren fire brightened the twilight. The enemy were further forward than expected, and were holding the area in strength. The Kangaroos and tanks pulled back, with bullets crashing like hail on their steel hides. The Cornish riflemen, remaining where they had dismounted, quickly went to the ground in hurriedly scraped holes, but then I got the advance going, but progress was slow. The terrain between B Coy and the autobahn was littered with trenches and dug cuts, each of which had to be carefully searched. A few Germans were winkled out, very frightened and anxious to be 'by-passed'.

Adding to our problems were several deep dykes, about 8 ft wide, crossing these obstacles took time, and the Germans took the opportunity of bombarding them heavily with mortars. Fortunately, their aim for most of the time was inaccurate.

Our casualties were relatively light, but the long drawn out advance through the night was tiring everyone. Considerable small arms fire could be heard to our right, where the Somerset's were fighting in the woods near Vehlingen.

Shapes of buildings ahead were identified as the houses south of Boevesaig. A heavy 'stonk' of artillery fire was directed at them, covering the company's advance at the same time.

Some 20 Germans who had been sleeping in the cellar of one building gave themselves up without a struggle. But three others bravely tried reaching for their rifles. The rambling buildings contained more defenders than we had thought, but by 4 am the men of B Coy were firmly established. At first light, the farm at Boevesiag became visible across the flat country and Megchelin could be seen on the slight reverse slope. A good dyke bank provided cover to Boevesiag, and a patrol promptly moved forward to occupy it. C Coy were now able to move through, via the woods to the right of the bridge on their way to Megchelin. I was well forward, hoping to catch the enemy on the hop, but as we approached the belf of wire, the village was like a disturbed bee hive, with Germans in various stages of undress rushing to man their trenches.

I thought: "Oh Hell, we've missed surprising them!" Now it would mean a delay while we drew up a fire plan. Suddenly, I saw a troop of Lothian's Horse flame throwers advancing towards me. I quote the later report of the young officer leading them. "I came across the colonel of the 5th DCLI whom we had been detailed to support. He was a tall, ruddy faced man and said: 'Where the hell' had I been, and ordered me to attack at once." This they did most gallantly using flame. In a very short time the enemy surrendered . . . thus, the terror weapons saved both British and German lives. In the 'bag' went 60 paratroops and Luftwaffe personnel. It was during this short action that the indomitable Major Kitchen received his third wound of the campaign . . . in the leg. Later 'Kitch' was to receive a well merited DSO for his courageous and tenacious leadership.

But then came the retaliation, overturnes to a counter-attack, we thought. The enemy threw everything they had at Megchelin and its approaches . . . heavy artillery, medium and light shells, ack-ack and mortars.

We made good use of the recently vacated German trenches and concentrated on digging ourselves in deeper. With information provided by Dutch civilians, who had been sheltering in their cellars, we drove more Germans from their hiding places, and our 'bag' of prisoners steadily increased. We then consolidated the position. The going was certainly hot, with mortar concentrations from the forward edge to the centre of the village particularly fierce.

B Coy headquarters received a direct hit, but fortunately there were no casualties. During the late afternoon, 130 Bde, operating on an eastern axis just south of the village, pushed the enemy back further to the east and the Recce Regt moved in to the north; Megchelin soon became a back area.

After the battle, I visited the advanced dressing station, which we were sharing with a battalion from another brigade. I was surprised to see some 20 men of this battalion lying on stretchers, but with no signs of wounds.

The medical officer told me they were 'bomb happy' . . . battle exhaustion cases. I was horrified that their CO and medical officer could allow such a situation to develop.

In 5DCLI we had about 10 cases in the whole campaign. We had a method of preventing men from taking the easy way out. We had a system that exhausted men what ever the reason were not evacuated outside the battalion. They were sent to 'B' Echelon the transport lines and given sleeping pills and rested. They were normally back with their companies within 24 hours. A few stand backs were if this did not work kept at battalion headquarters doing fatigues . . . strangely I noticed that they had developed yellow complexions.

Megchelin was a fair example of the sort of resistance we were to meet in our advance into the interior of the Third Reich. The German paras and SS troops had fought hard, and the battalion had taken 94 prisoners. But this was the last time we would meet such a storm of artillery and mortar fire. Now, our advances were to become more continuous as the defence became more scattered.

CHAPTER TWELVE

Wagnerian Intermezzo

The German's attempt to contain us in a bridgehead had failed. Now, 30 Corps started on its long lunge forward to capture Bremen. The Guards Armoured Division were to make the main thrust, along an axis comprised of Groente, Enschede, Quackenbruck and Bremen.

We of 43 Div were to provide left flank protection for the Corps, and 3 Div were to follow the Guards as immediate corps reserve. The 51 Highland Div were to rest.

The advance was to be sustained night and day. This meant that every division of 30 Corps would move forward on a one-brigade front, with each brigade fighting its way out of any trouble encountered. Then the next brigade would pass through to keep up the momentum of the attack.

A brigade, therefore, would have to fight and move for four or five days before the next one took up the running. Each battalion in turn was given the task of leading its respective brigade.

The leading battalion usually moved behind a screen of armoured cars and carriers of the Division Recce Regt, with a mixed company group consisting of four or five tanks and 10 armoured Kangaroos, carrying infantry, sections and 3 inch mortars and anti-tank guns.

Then came the commanding group, with the CO and his artillery, tank and engineering officers. Behind them were further company groups of tanks, Kangaroos and Churchill flame-throwers, followed up by a seemingly endless column of the rest of the brigade, division tanks, lorries full of infantrymen, artillery ammunition lorries, Engineers with their Bailey and Scissor bridges, and ambulances ominously in the rear.

The long armoured column clattered and clanked its way like some giant centipede across the Dutch-German border, its obvious power heartening the Hollanders and depressing the Reich volk.

Brigadier Essame told me that when the turn of 5DCLI came to lead the division he was going to use us for the night advances to undermine any attempt by the enemy to consolidate their defensive positions. Tribute, indeed, to the battalion's aptitude for this type of operation, which we had proved in such places as Le Plessis Grimault Goch and Driel, near Arnhem. but the brigadier's proposal was received with somewhat wry smiles by our hardened veterans.

A succession of towns and villages fell relentlessly into the divisions net, but not without a struggle. For the Germans' paratroopers were still presenting a co-ordinated, if somewhat thin, defence, and as they fell back they were blowing every bridge with remorseless efficiency and blocking roads with great timbered obstructions.

Easter, 1945, was indeed a time of hope; we advanced over 50 miles through Holland during the six day period. Easter Sunday, although cold and raw, was a day of great jubilation.

The Dutch, on their way to church to celebrate the risen Christ, gave us a great welcome, bringing a lump to the throat and tears to eye of many a bold warrior. It was, indeed, a sight to behold: throughout the day,

> **"the roads, villages and town were lined with waving, cheering people: old men in blue caps with knobbly sticks, their wives in laundered white bonnets of linen; pretty girls with orange bows in their hair, and children with orange flowers, symbolic of the royal House of Orange. Young men with shovels, filling in the holes and tank ruts with turf cut from the roadside. And above the roar of the vehicles passing by, the happy shouts of 'Hallo, Tommy!'"**

At Hengle, the battalion moved into billets south of the canal, while the enemy still held the north bank. We were sniped at and mortared as we moved into the area of the salt factory, but none of us paid much heed; our main concern was bed and board after a long cold and tiring day.

The noise of battle could be heard clearly from the town as

130 Bde attacked it from the east, but, protected by our outposts, we were soon peacefully asleep. Hengle duly fell. Our Pioneers spent the next day clearing mines, and before nightfall the Sappers had thrown up a bridge over the canal. Next day we relieved the 1st Suffolk's at Oldenzaal, a town undamaged by the war where we duly refreshed ourselves in the public baths. The news was good: the Guards and 3 Div had taken Lingen, a bottle-neck on the Ems River and the Dortmund-Ems Canal. We left friendly Holland and moved over the border into Germany, to Nordhorn, a cotton manufacturing town.

From the windows of the houses hung the limp, white flags of a sullen, defeated nation, in contrast to the yellow welcoming flags of Holland. We passed a peaceful and comfortable night in this prosperous and undamaged town.

April 7, and into the final month of war. It was bitterly cold for the time of the year and we were glad to curl up in a wood protecting us from the cutting wind as we moved in the direction of Lingen.

At dawn came the word to move on: our brigade was to lead the division. This meant we would take the brunt of any action, as we forced the crossing of the River Hase with the intention of capturing Haselunne.

Shortly before midday, the long column halted, and we heard that 7 Somerset's, who were in the vanguard, were held up by road blocks near the village of Bawinkel. These were quickly demolished by Petard tanks.

But the enemy were holding the main road into the town in some strength. It was decided that while the Somerset's seized a crossing at Buckelte, 5th Cornwall's would move along the road to Haselunne to provide a decoy for the main attack.

From the church tower at Bawinkel, I surveyed the situation with my company commanders. The church itself was being used as a refuge by the German villagers, and I agreed they could stay as long as they behaved themselves.

In the early spring sunlight we could clearly see the large wood, with its emerging green foliage, which shielded Haseluune from our view. The road at its edge was blocked by a whole row of trees, which had been neatly dropped by explosive charges. I decided then not only to put in a holding attack, but to destroy the enemy rearguard facing us. The outline plan catered for a 'holding fire' attack by D Coy, a main effort right inner hook by A and B Coys, and an outer right hook by Holly Holland's C Coy, supported by tanks of 13/18 Hussars and a forward observation officer RA. It was considered that wireless sets would be vital to the success of the operation. D Coy quickly established itself in the area of a farmhouse just off the road, with the 3 in mortar and machine gun platoons and some anti-tank guns.

C Coy had already started its wide turning movement, and the two assaulting companies, who were to make the shorter enveloping move, had reached their forming-up positions. Now we would have to wait patiently while Holly's men completed their manoeuvre, with pressure from behind, Brigade understandably directing us to make a direct frontal assault to draw the enemy's attention from the Somerset's. Meanwhile, we kept the Germans occupied with mortar, Bren and machine gun fire.

At last came word that C Coy had reached it's forming-up point without incident. Then down went our barrage in front of D Coy, and the assault companies, supported by the tanks, dashed forward into the wood. Captain John Rabet's D Coy were firing in everything they had to cover the assault. Resistance was spasmodic. A great number of Germans lay dead, and the wood was full of wounded.

As D Coy started to advance, I moved with them. The pioneers quickly pronounced the felled trees clear of mines and a bulldozer was moved up to clear them.

In the wood, the assault companies were told to swing north . . . B Coy to the right of the road and A Coy to the left. D Coy with the Command Group then moved into the heart of the forest. It was now dark and small parties of Germans kept slipping across the road. Many of them were wounded, so we held our fire.

From the command post moving down the middle of the road I co-ordinated the advance as our twin-pronged vanguard pushed forward on either side.

With no moon, we worked in pitch darkness. Soon, the trees gave way to open space, several hundred yards of hummocks and bracken. A burst of fire and the noise of several bursting grenades shattered the darkness.

On we went, groping our way forward. What was this? We had reached another patch of woodland and a massive wall loomed in our path. It was another road block, composed of stout logs and shingle. A quick recce showed there was a minefield, too. Beyond the road-block, a small bridge over a stream had been blown. But there was good news, too. The scout Platoon had made contact with C Coy, with whom we had lost radio contact shortly after dark. They had unhinged the whole enemy defence with a wide detour, and were now covering a small footbridge that had remained intact. Plans were immediately made to take advantage of this and Captain Rabet was told to be prepared to move with D Coy before dawn and advance over the footbridge towards the River Loop, below Haselunne. But it was all to end in disaster. Guided by the Scout Patrol, the company set off in single file. But then, unaccountably, things went tragically wrong.

Evidently, there was some sort of misunderstanding between Rabet and his guides, for instead of turning right on to a track leading from the road he decided to push straight on to skirt the minefield. A blinding flash lit up the night, followed by the roar of an exploding mine. Gries of wounded men rent the air. Lieut Wheeler, whose platoon was holding position near the road-block, bravely rushed forward to offer assistance and was badly wounded when he triggered off another mine.

The wounded were finally brought out at great risk by their comrades of D Coy. But John Rabet, a most gallant and competent officer, was dead. His death confirmed an uncomfortable feeling that I had harboured since attending mass one Sunday morning in the little Catholic church at Cleve, during the battle of the Reichwald. I had seen John praying most earnestly, and I had the feeling he would not survive the war. Shortly before he was killed, he stood boldly in the road, only a short distance from the enemy. I told him not to be so foolish and to join me in the ditch. Later, when giving him orders, I was especially aware of my strange feeling and told him to be particularly careful, emphasising that the guide knew the ground well and that John Rabet should depend on him.

During the early morning, 5DCLI advanced a short distance, but was then told to stand fast until relieved by a battalion from 130 Bde. Soon, we were moving over the River Hase crossing earlier seized by the Somerset's. With the Haselunne captured by the Worcester's, we were able to relax for a few short hours in a small red-bricked hamlet.

Our respite was all too brief. Just before nightfall, we were ordered to move off to cross-roads, a few miles east of the captured town. We took over from a squadron of Recce Regt with little formality by the light of a burning barn, near a little hamlet.

Our patrols, supported by machine guns and mortars, kept close contact with the enemy, who withdrew just before dawn. Then 129 Bde passed through in hot pursuit and our little hamlet became a peaceful backwater . . . except for a constant stream of traffic.

This time, we had a respite from training, other than a tactical discussion, and time was spent sleeping or social visiting within the battalion.

We provided one cheery visitor, Lieut Col Algy Grubb CO of Worcester's, with useful first hand experiences for his Divisional Battle School, and John Stancombe invited our officers to help his squadron of 13/18 Hussars demolish their goodly supply of champagne. It was in this area that we first came across some of the Reich's Russian and Polish slave labourers and we wondered how many more we would find as we progressed farther east.

One of them complained that a big German farmer had misused him and beaten him. We arrested the farmer and I ordered the worker to give him six of the best across the backside. The man wanted to continue the punishment, but I resisted the temptation and stopped him.

CHAPTER THIRTEEN

End of War in Europe in Our Time?

While the rest of the division pushed on vigorously towards Cloppenburg, we spent our time mopping up enemy stragglers in the woods around Haselunne. Then, early on April 13, the battalion was on the move again. The 7th Hampshires had secured an unblown bridge over the river in the northern part of Cloppenburg, and the town, although still under enemy bombardment, was in our hands. We of 5DCLI were to exploit through this area in the direction of Ahlhorn.

With David Willcocks, I went forward into Cloppenburg to assess the situation before drawing up my battle plan. Parts of the town were a mess from the bombing and shelling, and some buildings were still on fire. Enemy mortar bombs and shells crashed wickedly around us, and above us air bursts added to the nightmarish pandemonium.

We located the Hampshire's battalion HQ in the cellar of a garage. Outside, the petrol pumps battered by shells, were sprawled like drunken sentinels. Companies of the Hampshires were reported to be mopping up around the town. Willcocks and I withdrew to a house two miles outside battered Cloppenburg, and I issued orders to the assembled company commanders and specialist officers of DCLI.

My plan was simple: B Coy, under Major Holland, would advance into the town and form a firm base of the eastern edge. From here, C Coy would do a night advance of some 3,000 yards to secure a start line on the railway track, from which A and B Coys would make a converging attack on a small feature called 'The Kidney'. Night was falling as Holland's men crossed the bridge in single file. Despite the earlier assurances of the Hampshires, it was becoming increasingly obvious that Cloppenburg, was by no means yet in British hands. The rapid staccato of numerous Spandaus, answered by the throaty roar of the Hampshires' Brens, could be heard intermingled with the noise of mortars and grenades. By skilled map reading, Holly was able to move his company forward into the shrubs. I joined them as soon as they encountered resistance, and, by the light of torches, we discussed our next move in a cellar in which some frightened German civilians were huddled.

I decided to back up our advance with tanks of the Sherwood Rangers, a rifle platoon of the 60th Rifles, and our wasp carrier section (Flame Thrower).

The advance continued slowly, with every house being searched. Bazookas inflicted some casualties on the tank and carrier crews, and the platoon commander of 60th Rifles was killed while gallantly leading his men against a strongly held house. On our right flank, the Hampshires were having a similar battle in the cold starlit night. But by 10 pm B Coy had gained their objective, and C Coy, with tank support, were able to launch their attack on the railway line.

But the Germans of the Gross Deutschland Division, Crack Formation, it was later learned, were still in no mood for surrendering. C Coy, having to clear every house, battled their way forward slowly, much to the consternation of A and D Coys, who were anxious to start operations on 'The Kidney' before daybreak.

At last, after eight wearying hours, Lieut Williams and his 14 Platoon reached the railway and the two companies crossed their start line only half an hour before dawn.

A Coy, on the right, braved the fire of several Spandaus to gain their initial objective. By now, the German spirit of resistance was breaking, and a whole company surrendered to D Coy on the left.

Daylight revealed the scenario of hordes of enemy prisoners being marched back from the village. But things were by no means over yet. A Panther tank rolled out of the woods to shoot up C Coy HQ at only 25 yards range. And the crew of a Valentine tank had a miraculous escape when an 88 shell went through one side and out the other.

Ironically, in this late skirmish the only casualty was a German sergeant, who had just become a prisoner of war, killed by his own side.

Settled comfortably in the now-captured town, we spent a pleasant day and night resting. Then, while the other two battalions of the brigade pushed on to secure the major crossroads and railway west of Ahlhorn, 5DCLI were busy clearing the woods around Cloppenburg. It was during this operation that Lieut Southworth was wounded and his driver killed when their carrier went up on a mine.

The only opposition came from 88 mm guns that the enemy were operating against the flanks of the main axis of the division's advance. These fired high explosive and solid shot that whistled about 10 ft over our heads. Our usual answer was to get our artillery to shell them heavily to stop them annoying us.

Meanwhile, the Somerset's and Worcester's were pushing forward along the road running through the great dark and gloomy forests of pine and spruce. Near Ahlhorn, 1 Worcester's repulsed a heavy counter attack in which the German infantry, cleverly supported by tanks, advanced in masse in 1914 style.

On April 16, 5DCLI were back in their role of the brigade's vanguard. On the outskirts of Ahlhorn, our patrols spotted about 10 Germans and we sensed that the enemy were withdrawing from the big village. But on the other hand, they could have been holding the place in strength, one cannot afford to rely on instinct when the lives of men are at stake.

A few well placed Spandaus could inflict many casualties in a few seconds; although the gunners would not like wasting precious ammunition at such a crucial time.

We decided to lay on a short, sharp artillery preparation. As our shells crashed down with loud clatters on the red tiled buildings, C and B Coy swept forward. It was more like manoeuvres back in Kent than the final stages of the war in Germany. The village was empty of enemy troops, and soon we were comfortably ensconced in the large red farm house, with outposts placed to the north and east to keep a wary eye on the scattered groups of German gunners and infantry.

We spent a pleasant two days at Ahlhorn, at one time entertaining the brigade commander to dinner in the pleasant village inn. We were elated by the news from the BBC that three armoured divisions were closing in on Hamburg. Now we knew that the end could not be far off.

On April 23, 5DCLI moved forward 40 miles to the outskirts of Bremen. The 43rd Division were to cross the Weser and clear the residential areas of the city after the initial assault by 52 and 53 divs.

We crossed the river early next morning at Haya. Here, the traffic on the road slowed down the column so I pushed on ahead in an armoured Dingo to contact 156 Bde (Ind) and 1 Glasgow Highlander's, from whom we were to take over. The recce regt of 52 Div had been out towards the autobahn and had met no resistance. It was decided to push forward quickly to the autobahn which had been our objective for the night. The companies caught me up at about midday and we reached the motorway late in the afternoon. Accompanied by the leading platoon commander of A Coy, I crept forward on to the flyover and surveyed the scene.

To the right was a pine forest and on the other side was open country, dotted with fine farms with big red tiled barns. Again the question: was the line of the autobahn to be held or not?

I decided again on a short, sharp fire plan to shield the initial attack. The Company went in, covered by concentrations of artillery fire and the Middlesex Regt machine guns.

The only resistance was spasmodic fire from a few 88s and mortars. Next day, by then firmly in command, we decided to blow the bridges across a stream northwest of the autobahn to protect the right flank of the division's thrust to Bremen. This the sappers carried out at night under the noses of the enemy. We codenamed this operation 'Blow' and it netted us a bonus of 12 prisoners of war. We were relieved at noon the next day by 2 Bn, The Black Watch, with the spring sun shinning as though it was midsummer. The assault on Bremen had started: 129 Bde was fighting its way towards the big Burgher Park, in which the underground defences HQ of the city was located. There was considerable fighting before the Wilts' and Dorset's, using flame throwers finally overcame the resistance and captured the garrison commander and the survivors of his SS force.

We spent the night billeted in the clean little suburban houses on the outskirts of the city. Next day, our task was to secure an exit across the Weser at the north end of Bremen for the division's drive to Bremerhaven.

The 1st Worcester's met little resistance in paving the way for us, but when we moved through them to find the bridge blown the plan was quickly changed. The Wessex division would hand over the city to 52 Div, then go back eastwards, to swing a right hook over the River Hunte and on to Bremerhaven.

It was to be 43 Div's last operation of the war. In the lead was 129 Bde, with 214 Bde protecting the left flank. We Cornwalls were on the right, the Somerset's on the left. The low, boggy country was intersected by dykes and streams, so we had to keep to the roads. The opposition was light, consisting mainly of a screen of Spandaus and Nebelwerfer mortars.

But these 'Moaning Minnies', as we called them, were manned by teams of instructors from the Nebelwerfer school, and their fire at all times was dealy accurate. But because of the noise the projectiles made, everyone had ample time to take cover, and casualties were mercifully few. It was not until late in the afternoon that the battalion made frontal contact with the enemy. We decided to attack after dark on a two company front, Captain Anslow's D Coy to the right and A Coy, commanded by Major Roberts to the left.

Opposition was spasmodic, and a steady flow of prisoners were taken throughout the night. Our objective was Grasberg, which, according to one prisoner, was being held by 200 German troops. I moved up to make contact with D Coy at dawn, and after a swift recce, we drew up plans for a fresh attack to be made just after breakfast. Occasional bursts of mortar and machine gun fire met us as we moved swiftly in open order through the wet grass of that spring morning. There were no casualties. It was the last opposition we were to encounter of the war.

We moved into Grasberg to find that the defenders had

fled. We had taken 74 prisoners in this final operation. Now we moved west to link up with 52 Div, who had rebuilt the bridges blown previously by us over the Wesser. A new sense of self-preservation had now entered our lives. We had felt for several days that the end of our long ordeal was now in sight and instinctively we became more cautious in our planning and personal movements.

We had come so far and been through so much that further sacrifices seemed unwarranted and unjustified. In those final stages, we did our job with the minimum of casualties.

It was while entertaining to dinner in Battalion HQ some Merchant Navy Officers freed from captivity that I received the signal on the night of May 5, 1945. I read it out: the northern group of German armies, consisting of 1½ million men, had surrendered to Montgomery, Hostilities would cease forthwith.

Rockets and tracer bullets criss crossed the night sky and the doors of the hut burst open and a flood of our men carried us shoulder high round the room into the night. I could not but reflect, "Was this the real end of war in our time?" combined with the deep feeling of gratitude to my officers, and men. I looked upon them as my sons. They had never failed and now thank God they could go back in due course to their families (1).

Note (1)

Some years later our Brigadier Essame (Major General) told me of a conversation that he had with General Sir Miles Dempsey commander of the 2nd Army about who were the best battalions in that Army and they came to the conclusion that they were the 1st Bn The East Lancashire Regt, and the 5th Duke of Cornwall's Light Infantry, as regards the latter their judgement was no doubt swayed to some extent by the very low numbers of 'battle fatigue cases', some 2% whilst the average was 8%.

The Battalion marching past Field Marshal Montgomery, just after the end of the war in Germany, headed on the right by Capt. Gorman MC, in the centre, Major Kitchen DSO and on the left of the column, Capt. Anslow MBE. The Colonel is a few yards ahead.